PRIDE AND PREJUDICE
BY JANE AUSTEN

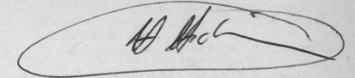

MACMILLAN MASTER GUIDES

General Editor: James Gibson

Published:
JANE AUSTEN: **PRIDE AND PREJUDICE** Raymond Wilson
       EMMA Norman Page
       MANSFIELD PARK Richard Wirdnam
ROBERT BOLT: **A MAN FOR ALL SEASONS** Leonard Smith
EMILY BRONTË: **WUTHERING HEIGHTS** Hilda D. Spear
GEOFFREY CHAUCER: **THE PROLOGUE TO THE CANTERBURY**
          TALES Nigel Thomas and Richard Swan
CHARLES DICKENS: **GREAT EXPECTATIONS** Dennis Butts
        HARD TIMES Norman Page
GEORGE ELIOT: **MIDDLEMARCH** Graham Handley
      SILAS MARNER Graham Handley
OLIVER GOLDSMITH: **SHE STOOPS TO CONQUER** Paul Ranger
THOMAS HARDY: **FAR FROM THE MADDING CROWD**
       Colin Temblett-Wood
CHRISTOPHER MARLOWE: **DOCTOR FAUSTUS** David A. Male
GEORGE ORWELL: **ANIMAL FARM** Jean Armstrong
WILLIAM SHAKESPEARE: **MACBETH** David Elloway
         A MIDSUMMER NIGHT'S DREAM
         Kenneth Pickering
         ROMEO AND JULIET Helen Morris
         THE WINTER'S TALE Diana Devlin

Forthcoming:
GEOFFREY CHAUCER: **THE MILLER'S TALE** Michael Alexander
T. S. ELIOT: **MURDER IN THE CATHEDRAL** Paul Lapworth
E. M. FORSTER: **A PASSAGE TO INDIA** Hilda D. Spear
WILLIAM GOLDING: **THE SPIRE** Rosemary Sumner
THOMAS HARDY: **TESS OF THE D'URBERVILLES** James Gibson
HARPER LEE: **TO KILL A MOCKINGBIRD** Jean Armstrong
       THE METAPHYSICAL POETS Joan van Emden
ARTHUR MILLER: **THE CRUCIBLE** Leonard Smith
GEORGE BERNARD SHAW **ST JOAN** Leonee Ormond
WILLIAM SHAKESPEARE: **HAMLET** Jean Brooks
         HENRY IV PART ONE Helen Morris
         JULIUS CAESAR David Elloway
         KING LEAR Francis Casey
         OTHELLO Christopher Beddowes
         TWELFTH NIGHT Edward Leeson
RICHARD SHERIDAN: **THE RIVALS** Jeremy Rowe
        THE SCHOOL FOR SCANDAL Paul Ranger
JOHN WEBSTER: **THE DUCHESS OF MALFI/THE WHITE DEVIL**
       David A. Male

Also published by Macmillan

MACMILLAN MASTER SERIES

Mastering English Literature R. Gill
Mastering English Language S. H. Burton
Mastering English Grammar S. H. Burton

MACMILLAN MASTER GUIDES
PRIDE AND PREJUDICE
BY JANE AUSTEN

RAYMOND WILSON

MACMILLAN

First edition 1985

Published by
MACMILLAN EDUCATION LTD
Houndmills, Basingstoke, Hampshire RG21 2XS
and London
Companies and representatives
throughout the world

Printed in Hong Kong

ISBN 0-333-37428-2 Pbk
ISBN 0-333-39471-2 Pbk export

CONTENTS

GENERAL EDITOR'S PREFACE

The aim of the Macmillan Master Guides is to help you to appreciate the book you are studying by providing information about it and by suggesting ways of reading and thinking about it which will lead to a fuller understanding. The section on the writer's life and background has been designed to illustrate those aspects of the writer's life which have influenced the work, and to place it in its personal and literary context. The summaries and critical commentary are of special importance in that each brief summary of the action is followed by an examination of the significant critical points. The space which might have been given to repetitive explanatory notes has been devoted to a detailed analysis of the kind of passage which might confront you in an examination. Literary criticism is concerned with both the broader aspects of the work being studied and with its detail. The ideas which meet us in reading a great work of literature, and their relevance to us today, are an essential part of our study, and our Guides look at the thought of their subject in some detail. But just as essential is the craft with which the writer has constructed his work of art, and this is considered under several technical headings - characterisation, language, style and stagecraft.

The authors of these Guides are all teachers and writers of wide experience, and they have chosen to write about books they admire and know well in the belief that they can communicate their admiration to you. But you yourself must read and know intimately the book you are studying. No one can do that for you. You should see this book as a lamppost. Use it to shed light, not to lean against. If you know your text and know what it is saying about life, and how it says it, then you will enjoy it, and there is no better way of passing an examination in literature.

JAMES GIBSON

ACKNOWLEDGEMENTS

Cover illustration: *English Landscape with a house* by Heywood Hardy.
© Roy Miles Fine Paintings, London, Courtsey of the Bridgeman Art Library.

1 JANE AUSTEN:
LIFE AND BACKGROUND

1.1 JANE AUSTEN'S LIFE

Jane Austen was born in 1775 at Steventon in Hampshire of middle-class parents. George Austen, her father, was an Oxford graduate without personal fortune. He supplemented his income as rector of Steventon by taking pupils, alongside whom he would teach his own children. As the seventh child in the family, Jane was educated in part by her older brothers, two of whom were to become clergymen, while two others rose to the rank of admiral in the Navy, and yet another, Edward, was through adoption made a member of the landed gentry. The wide range of activities within the Austen family – country walks, charades, reading, writing stories and family plays – constituted a rich informal education for the children, and stimulated Jane Austen's ambition to become a novelist. Her formal education at boarding schools in Oxford, Southampton and Reading was certainly brief and relatively unimportant.

While in her teens, and learning her craft as a novelist, Jane Austen shrewdly observed the rural community among whom she lived, and attended such social activities as the fashionable balls held in nearby towns. Neither she nor her devoted sister, Cassandra, married. Cassandra was engaged, but her fiancé was tragically drowned; Jane herself became engaged to a friend of her brother's, only to break off the engagement next day. Unlike Charlotte Lucas in *Pride and Prejudice*, she was unwilling to marry someone she did not love for the sake of status, security and a home of her own.

Her father retired in 1801 and the family moved to Bath, a city less fashionable than it had been half a century before. Jane Austen was never happy there, nor in Southampton, where they moved in 1805, after her father's death; but in 1809 her brother Edward offered his mother and sisters a small country house at Chawton, on his Hampshire estate. It was here that Jane Austen, now a favourite maiden aunt with her brother's children, wrote and revised earlier work, achieving sufficient literary success to attract the attention of the Prince Regent, to whom *Emma* was dedicated when it was published in 1815.

During 1816 Jane Austen became an invalid and in May 1817 she took lodgings in Winchester, to be near a good doctor; but at that time little could be done for Addison's disease, from which she died on 18th July 1817. A devout Christian, she was buried in Winchester Cathedral.

1.2 THE GENERAL BACKGROUND

Jane Austen lived through a turbulent period of our history. During most of her adult life, Britain was at war with revolutionary France (1793-1815), while at home a traditional agricultural economy and culture was being gradually transformed by a rapidly developing industrial revolution. The aristocratic eighteenth century was challenged by radical political thinkers, who argued for greater democracy, and a new evangelism, far removed from formal religion, spread a living faith among all sections of society, including the new industrial working class.

The fact is, however, that none of this is portrayed in the novels. What Jane Austen needed, as a novelist, was not the broad canvas of Europe torn apart by the Napoleonic wars, but, as she herself wrote, '3 or 4 Families in a Country Village'. If she makes a vague mention of peace in the last chapter of *Pride and Prejudice*, she does so, not because of any importance in the event itself, but because it gives Lydia and Wickham an opportunity to set up a home of their own. It may well be that Jane Austen was brought into contact with broader, more public issues than her novels deal with, but as a writer she deliberately restricts herself to portraying the commonplace events of people of her own class, living quiet, rural lives that are barely touched by the momentous happenings of history. Even the Industrial Revolution is ignored, except in so far as it is implied in the portrayal of such a character as Bingley, who has no settled family estate and wishes to emulate well-established gentry like Darcy by buying one out of the fortune made by his father in the North – that is, in such cities as Manchester and Liverpool, where there was a rapid expansion of grim, industrial slums.

What the novels do painstakingly portray is the social scene of the well-to-do rural classes, whose standards inevitably seem remote and rigid to us. The upper and middle classes of the period were organised on traditional, hierarchical principles. In general, people remained in the station in life into which they were born, and though by hard work an exceptional individual might make a fortune in trade or the new industries, the social tone was set by the landed gentry, proud of their ancient ancestry and homes. The moral code was clearly defined and much more severely applied than our own. Manners and speech were more elaborate and formal than ours now are. In the best society, men managed their estates, but otherwise they did not work, while the only recognised success in life available to a woman was to marry well.

The cultural background to the novels is also of importance. Jane Austen's life coincides approximately with the first phase of the great shift in culture we call Romanticism. The eighteenth century boasted it was the Age of Reason and Enlightenment. Men believed that they lived in 'the best of possible worlds' and that science both explained the design of the universe and held out the hope of indefinite progress for the future. According to this tidy view of life, art, nature and human nature could all be explained by rational principles, and the head was held to prevail over the heart. The Romantic Movement attempted to reverse this by championing intuition, the emotions and the imagination, in opposition to the tyranny of the intellect. The strength of the Age of Reason lay in its balanced judgement, its restraint, its good sense and good taste, all of which matter enormously in the work of Jane Austen, who is rather backward-looking in the values she affirms. But, as she well knew, these values could be perverted into deadening and inflexible conformity. The strength of Romanticism lay in its reverence for the emotions and personal intuition, and Jane Austen respects and realises this. But Romanticism tends to sensationalism, egotism and eccentricity, and she brings her eighteenth-century good sense and satire to bear on all such excesses.

In literature, these excesses were conspicuously found in the so-called Gothic novels, the most popular fiction of the period. They were potboilers of extreme violence and sadism, designed to make flesh creep with their improbable heroines undergoing nightmarish adventures in ivied ruins in desolate wastes haunted by the ghosts of long-dead nuns and monks. In another early novel, *Northanger Abbey*, Jane Austen splendidly burlesques and ridicules these romances, but in *Pride and Prejudice* she deliberately gives us a novel at the opposite extreme from such fiction. It is domestic, confined, unadventurous and restrained. The values it affirms are basically those of the eighteenth century at its best – practical good sense, good taste, civilised respect for other people – but there is also a recognition that the individual matters as an individual and that sincere and genuine feelings are of paramount importance, and this recognition draws on what is best in the Romantic tradition.

1.3 THE WORLD OF *PRIDE AND PREJUDICE*

We have noted that Jane Austen herself speaks of a country village as an ideal setting for her novels, and the writer Sir Walter Scott was quick to see that, even allowing for this, she concentrates on only a narrow section of society:

> . . . [she] confines herself chiefly to the middling classes of society; her most distinguished characters do not rise greatly above well-bred gentlemen and ladies; and those which are sketched with most originality and precision, belong to a class rather below that standard. (1826)

While Lady Catherine de Bourgh may claim to be an aristocrat, we should not overlook the fact that she emerges less as a character than a caricature. Meanwhile, it is true that servants, and even more, agricultural workers, though both were plentifully in the background of her characters' lives, hardly qualify for so much as a mention by the author. Mrs Hill, the housekeeper at Longbourn, and Mrs Reynolds, housekeeper at Pemberley, are wholly undeveloped characters; indeed, Mrs Reynolds is best defined as a device for conveying information about her master.

Though almost wholly preoccupied with 'the middling classes', Jane Austen further narrows her scope by disregarding many of their distinctive activities, such as hunting, shooting, and talking about politics and religion. The world of *Pride and Prejudice* is very nearly exclusively a world of manners and social convention. If we have any doubt as to what the codes and rules governing conduct and society are, when most severe, we can turn to Lady Catherine de Bourgh. Society is, for her, rigidly hierarchical. She has been born privileged, she lives a life that exacts subservience from her subordinates, and she believes that nothing – neither money, talent, beauty or love – should be allowed to disturb a social order so much to her advantage. What we probably think of as the accident or lottery of birth, she regards as the single most important determinant in life. The social hierarchy is for her part of the 'natural' order of the universe. It constitutes a 'pecking order' that is often respected by those who are not its most privileged members. Mr Collins, for example, while all servility towards his patron, is ridiculously condescending to his cousins, who are less well off than himself.

Fixed conventions govern the whole of the social life Jane Austen portrays and her characters are presented, sometimes approvingly, sometimes disapprovingly, as conforming to or deviating from them. Jane Austen can oppose convention, as Elizabeth Bennet does by refusing to defer to Lady Catherine's dictates; equally, she can conform to it, as Elizabeth does in reacting with horror to her sister's elopement and (as used to be said) 'living in sin'. Christian charity does nothing to soften Mr Collins's conventional reaction to Lydia's elopement, even though he is a clergyman: 'the death of your daughter would have been a blessing in comparison of this,' he tells Mr Bennet, by way of consoling him. But, of course, convention, which is often concerned for no more than appearances, can be lenient, too. Once Lydia and Wickham are married, society at large (though not Lady Catherine or Collins) is prepared to turn a blind eye to their former disgrace. Lady Catherine would insist that if the younger Bennet sisters had not been allowed to 'come out' until after their older sisters were married (following traditional convention), the elopement could never have happened, and they would have eventually secured better husbands from having acquired a more extensive education in art, music and needlework.

Pride and Prejudice involves us in a severely restricted and conventional world, but our amusement as readers comes from the author's exploration of this world in its minutest details. That Jane Austen is far from uncritically accepting convention is apparent from her making Elizabeth Bennet her heroine – and one she approved of as 'delightful'. Elizabeth refuses to feel shame for being unable to draw; though without fortune or security, she turns down advantageous offers of marriage; she actually blushes for Lydia and Wickham *after* they are 'respectably' married; and she has the spirit not to defer to that model of all that is conventional, Lady Catherine herself, since she is unimpressed by 'the stateliness of money and rank', dissociated from 'extraordinary talents' and virtue. This is, of course, to affirm a moral perspective, a set of values that matter very much more than conventions. In the end, Jane Austen, who owes much to her reading of Dr Johnson and numerous moral and religious writers of the eighteenth century, can be seen to be herself a moralist; but far from being solemnly didactic in the manner of the 'sentimental' novelists of the period, she affirms her serious moral convictions through a comedy of manners, through realistic social satire, through vividly created and amusing characters, and through her unremitting irony and wit.

Pride and Prejudice presents us with a world that is selective and extremely restricted. But there is a strength in this. The deliberately chosen limitations allow the author perfect control of her materials. She sets out to write a comedy of manners with total economy and brilliantly succeeds because her narrow range is made to serve artistic ends. The novel is very nearly perfect and has hardly a superfluous incident, action, character or word - a truth never better expressed than by the philosopher and critic George Henry Lewes in 1862:

> There are heights and depths in human nature Miss Austen has never scaled nor fathomed, there are worlds of passionate existence into which she has never set foot; but although this is obvious to every reader, it is equally obvious that she has risked no failures by attempting to delineate that which she has not seen. Her circle may be restricted, but it is complete. Her world is a perfect orb, and vital.

But so high an order of artistic achievement had to be laboriously worked at, and was the result of years of apprenticeship, dating back to her teenage efforts to write parody. *Pride and Prejudice* grew out of a first version entitled *First Impressions*, which was begun in 1796, but has not survived. Letters play an important role in *Pride and Prejudice* and it is likely that the first version was a story unfolded through the exchange of letters between the characters - a typical eighteenth-century novelist's device. We can reasonably assume that in *First Impressions* Jane Austen parodied the sentimental novels of her period. They portrayed mysterious heroes and swooning heroines, overwhelmed by love for one another at first sight, but by the time Jane Austen worked through several drafts and revisions, which was her practice, we are given a novel that radically transforms the elements of sentimental fiction and turns upside down the love-at-first-sight convention. Elizabeth is better fitted for playful and witty conversation than for swooning on a sofa; Darcy is more a snob than a man of mystery; and their first impressions involve dislike, rather than attraction. Moreover, first impressions are shown to be misleading and wrong. They become part of the theme of appearance and reality, which plays so important a part in the novel's conception.

But Jane Austen was not content simply to satirise sentimental fiction or the didactic novels which heavy-handedly opposed sentiment by presenting characters who were models of correct conduct and morality. *Pride and Prejudice* outgrew its burlesque beginnings to become a novel of realistic social satire, with complex human beings, not stereotypes, for its principal characters: it is set in everyday reality, not in the world of extraordinary circumstances and melodrama, and has claims to be the first truly modern novel.

1.4 A NOTE ON THE NOVELS

Of Jane Austen's novels, three were reworked from the time when she began them in her youth or young womanhood. They are *Sense and Sensibility* (1811), *Pride and Prejudice* (1813), and *Northanger Abbey* (1817). *Mansfield Park* (1814), *Emma* (1816) and *Persuasion* (published together with *Northanger Abbey* in 1817) are all works of her maturity. However, we must remember that, by the time of their publication, even those novels having an early origin had undergone major revision and *Northanger Abbey*, finally published in 1817, is stylistically fully mature. *Pride and Prejudice* was anonymous when it appeared in January 1813 in a three-volume edition, as was usual then. It was so well received by critics and the public that a second edition was brought out in November of the same year.

2 SUMMARIES

AND

CRITICAL COMMENTARY

Chapter 1

Summary

We are introduced to the Bennet household. Mrs Bennet is excited by the news that Mr Bingley, a bachelor, is moving into the neighbourhood. With five unmarried daughters, her mind is preoccupied with finding husbands for them, and Mr Bingley would clearly be an excellent 'catch'.

Commentary

The introduction to a novel is vitally important: it should give some indication of the theme and grip the reader's attention. These conditions are admirably fulfilled here. The very first sentence establishes the dominant theme of marriage, and does so with wit. It is a generalisation of the kind found in Dr Johnson and the eighteenth-century moralist tradition, and combines the ring of truth with irony. The reader's involvement is achieved by the use made of dialogue, rather than description and report, and the dialogue itself amuses because it so tellingly reveals the characters. Mrs Bennet is obviously an empty-headed hypochondriac; her husband is no less obviously a tease, especially at his wife's expense. They are hardly a good advertisement for marriage, yet they both assume it to be necessary for their daughters.

Chapter 2

Summary

Mr Bennet visits Mr Bingley promptly, but conceals his having done so until the evening, when he makes a teasingly gradual confession. Mrs Bennet and her daughters continue to talk about Mr Bingley, and Mr Bennet skilfully manipulates their discussion so that his news will contradict their expectations and astonish them.

Commentary

We are given additional insight into the characters of Mr and Mrs Bennet. Only after provoking his wife into exclaiming that she is 'sick of Bingley' will Mr Bennet admit to his visit, then quickly make a fine exit, 'fatigued with the raptures of his wife'. She, meanwhile, is thoroughly resentful towards her husband and projects her irritation on to her daughter, Kitty, who gets the sharp edge of her tongue for coughing; but immediately on learning that Mr Bennet has called on Bingley, she praises him as 'an excellent father' and is all benevolence towards everyone. We are afforded some insight into the sheer uneventfulness of the lives of the middle classes of this period: a newcomer in the neighbourhood is a preoccupying source of excitement in lives that tend to monotony.

Chapter 3

Summary

Mr Bennet eludes the skill of his wife and daughters in their attempts to find out more about Bingley from him: they have, therefore, to content themselves with local gossip and a glimpse of him from an upstairs window, when he returns Mr Bennet's visit and is kept in the study. However, Bingley attends a ball at Meryton, and Mrs Bennet and her daughters can finally satisfy their curiosity. Bingley is everything he ought to be: handsome, easy in manner, likeable. He has brought from London his two sisters; Mr Hurst, the husband of one of them; and a close friend, Mr Darcy. The report that Mr Darcy has ten thousand pounds annual income predisposes everyone to regard him as fine, tall, handsome and noble; in fact, he initially outshines Bingley in person, just as he does in income. But the company at the ball, once they discover Darcy to be aloof and hard to please, take offence, abruptly turn against him, and are as quick to condemn as formerly to praise him. Bingley, who is as easy as Darcy is difficult to please, tries to get his friend to enter into the spirit of the ball and to dance with Elizabeth Bennet; but Darcy rudely and pointedly declines. Bingley returns to dancing with Jane Bennet, to whom he is attracted, and Elizabeth, apparently more amused than hurt by Darcy's snubbing her, entertains her friends by giving them an account of it, even though it is against herself. When Mrs Bennet and her daughters return to Longbourn, they find Mr Bennet still up. For all his pretence of indifference, he is anxious to have an account of the evening.

Commentary

We are introduced to Bingley and Darcy, but within a framework of irony.
Bingley is presented as the ideal 'catch'. Darcy, however, has twice his
income, and *therefore* eclipses his friend in the opinion of society. However, once society discovers he considers himself above them, they rapidly
restore Bingley to their favour and find the qualities they have just admired
in Darcy to be wholly disagreeable. The deceptiveness of appearances and
first impressions, which is a recurrent theme in the novel, is encountered
here for the first time, and it is clear that Jane Austen is far from endors-
ing the view that the judgements of society are either sensible or reliable.
Elizabeth's first encounter with Darcy is more than enough to establish his
pride and initiate her prejudice. The device of eavesdropping was a convention frequently used by novelists of the period, but its use here, in a novel
that is in general cogently naturalistic, is neither happy nor convincing.
Given that Elizabeth is within earshot of Darcy, it is extremely unlikely
that Bingley, who is entirely good natured, would draw Darcy's attention
to her in a voice loud enough to be heard. But Darcy's reply, made after
he has caught Elizabeth's eye and lowered his own, is so gratuitously insulting as to be scarcely credible, for surely he would have lowered his voice
along with his eyes. It is difficult not to see this scene, so crucial to the
development of the whole plot, as a curious blemish in a novel that otherwise approximates to perfection.

Chapter 4

Summary

We are given an analysis of the characters introduced in the previous chapter. Bingley's excellent qualities and good breeding are admired by Jane
and admitted by Elizabeth; his manners are presented as a foil to Darcy's,
which continually give offence. Elizabeth, more critical than Jane, sees
through Bingley's sisters, who are the worst sort of snobs.

Commentary

The sweetness and modesty of Jane's character are apparent from her
charitable judgements and from her being surprised at Bingley's asking her
to dance a second time. Like Bingley, she is unspoiled and well disposed
towards everybody, and what she says is sincere, simple and unqualified
by wit. Elizabeth's speech, by contrast, is clever and epigrammatic. Typically, Elizabeth remarks that 'compliments always take *you* by surprise,
and *me* never'. But if compliments never surprise Elizabeth, it is because
she has a just appreciation of her own worth, and for this very reason she

is unlikely to forgive Darcy's snub. By making it ridiculous, she can preserve her good opinion of herself. Meanwhile, we have the author's word for it that Darcy is clever and of superior understanding to Bingley: 'In understanding, Darcy was the superior'.

Chapter 5

Summary
The events of the ball are further scrutinised when Lady Lucas, the wife of Sir William, whose knighthood has gone to his head, visits Longbourn with her daughter Charlotte. Mrs Bennet, conscious of Bingley's having honoured Charlotte by dancing with her first, seeks to be one up by virtually forcing Charlotte into recounting what she had heard Bingley remark to Mr Robinson about Jane's being the prettiest girl at the ball. The whole company are agreed that Darcy is eaten up with pride.

Commentary
Our pleasure in reading Jane Austen springs not only from the verbal wit of her characters, but from her own authorial wit. Of Sir William's knighthood she observes: 'The distinction had perhaps been felt too strongly', while the feather-brained Lady Lucas is introduced to us as a woman 'not too clever to be a valuable neighbour to Mrs Bennet'. Nor should one miss the author's amused moral condemnation of her characters, as when Mrs Bennet attributes Darcy's not speaking to Mrs Long to the fact that she 'does not keep a carriage'. In the very act of condemning Darcy's snobbishness, she is snobbishly congratulating herself on actually having the carriage Mrs Long lacks. The jest about Elizabeth's being 'only just *tolerable*' reveals an intimacy and cheerful friendship between Charlotte and Elizabeth, and some insight is given into Charlotte's very practical nature when she claims Darcy's pride does not offend *her*, 'because there is an excuse for it' in terms of his family and fortune. Finally, the amusement of the chapter is enhanced by Mary, whom the author satirises by making her talk pretentiously and sententiously, like a heavyweight book.

Chapter 6

Summary
The affection between Jane and Bingley continues to grow as visits are made between Netherfield and Longbourn, but Elizabeth remains unconvinced of the regard for Jane expressed by Bingley's sisters. She is relieved that Jane's subdued manner keeps her from betraying her love for Bingley

to the envy and criticism of society, and says as much to Charlotte Lucas, whose views about 'fixing' a husband and about marriage in general are wittily but cynically stated. Elizabeth rejects such cynicism and does not properly credit what Charlotte says. Meanwhile, Darcy surprises himself by discovering that he is increasingly attracted to Elizabeth. The Lucas's give a party which she attends and he reveals some interest in her. She however, is convinced that he is implacably disapproving of her and, from prejudice, misinterprets his actions and words alike. The blundering Sir William, after a mild snubbing from Darcy, presents Elizabeth to him as a dance partner. Darcy is 'not unwilling' but Elizabeth, remembering how he had so rudely rejected the suggestion that he should dance with her at the Netherfield ball, doggedly refuses. When Elizabeth escapes from him, Darcy is approached by Miss Bingley, who is jealously aware of the attraction Elizabeth has for him, and who tries to undo it by snobbishly pointing out the provincial narrowness and social deficiencies of their company. Darcy frankly admits to his liking for Elizabeth and her 'fine eyes'. Miss Bingley, affecting astonishment, declares sarcastically that Darcy 'will have a charming mother-in-law' in the vulgar and empty-headed Mrs Bennet.

Commentary

The marriage debate between Elizabeth and Charlotte is central to the whole book. Elizabeth's relief that Jane's discretion removes the possibility of gossip is challenged by Charlotte's perception that such discretion might also remove the possibility of a husband, since men need to be actively encouraged. Charlotte's recipe for marriage is, first fix your man; later there 'will be leisure for falling in love'. But married love is hardly taken seriously by her either. 'Happiness in marriage is entirely a matter of choice,' Charlotte declares, and she goes on to argue that 'it is better to know as little as possible of the defects of the person with whom you are to pass your life'. Elizabeth laughs at this, convinced that Charlotte would never act so calculatingly. Marriage for Elizabeth implies more than landing a rich husband: affection, character, mutual understanding are necessary, too. Ironically, she is blind to any token of interest or affection on Darcy's part, and mocks him by declaring that he 'is all politeness'. She is too set on demonstrating to him that she is *not* looking for a partner to notice that he would genuinely like to dance with her. We are made aware of a certain high seriousness in Darcy. He is filled with 'silent indignation' at the mindless way in which some of the company prefer dancing 'to the exclusion of all conversation'; but his indignation subsides quickly enough when Sir William proposes he should himself dance with Elizabeth! Even when Darcy dismissively asserts 'every savage can dance', we recognise a turn of phrase and mind that has something in common with Elizabeth's cleverness and wit. Some affinity between them is apparent to the reader long before it is apparent to Elizabeth herself.

Chapter 7

Summary

The two youngest and silliest Bennet sisters, Catherine and Lydia, persistently visit their aunt, Mrs Phillips, in the nearby village of Meryton, drawn there by their interest in the officers of a militia regiment which has moved into the neighbourhood. A note is sent to Jane from Miss Bingley, inviting her to dine at Netherfield, and Mrs Bennet schemingly insists her daughter should go on horseback. As Mrs Bennet hoped, it rains, and Jane is obliged to stay the night. Next morning, she has a cold and sends a letter to Elizabeth, telling her that the Bingleys insist on her staying until she is better. Elizabeth sets out and walks the three miles to Netherfield to satisfy herself about Jane's health, and her appearance after her walk surprises everyone. Jane has a fever and Elizabeth sits with her in the bedroom. When Elizabeth attempts to return home, Jane is distressed and Miss Bingley, whose kindness to Jane has made Elizabeth think rather better of her, invites Elizabeth to stay at Netherfield until Jane recovers.

Commentary

The characters of Mr and Mrs Bennet are nicely illustrated by their views on Catherine and Lydia. For Mr Bennet they are 'two of the silliest girls in the country'. For his wife, her daughters 'are all of them very clever'. The fact that he is their father does not blind him to his daughters' faults, but it is wholly otherwise with Mrs Bennet, who asserts that if she wished 'to think slightingly of anybody's children, it should not be [her] own. . .'. With heavy sarcasm, Mr Bennet flatters himself that 'this is the only point . . .on which we do not agree'. The fact is, Mrs Bennet is as silly as Catherine and Lydia; her indulgence towards them comes from her still, at heart, liking a red-coat herself. However, she contrives to combine silliness with cunning. She calculates that it is likely to rain and deliberately sends Jane to Netherfield on horseback, reasoning that Jane may have to stay overnight, and so be in a position further to impress Bingley with her charms. Jane's cold comes as a bonus to Mrs Bennet's scheme, and her delight is matched only by Mr Bennet's contempt. If Jane should die, he observes, 'it would be a comfort to know that it was all in pursuit of Mr Bingley. . .'. But the chapter also affords us further insight into the characters of the older sisters. Jane is unprotesting and submissive to her mother's manipulations. Elizabeth defies her mother by insisting on walking to Netherfield. Her concern for Jane makes her indifferent to both convention and her own appearance. When 'with weary ankles, dirty stockings, and a face glowing' she is shown into the breakfast parlour at Netherfield, the varied responses of the company she finds there epitomise their characters: the Bingley sisters are contemptuously incredulous, their brother kind and understanding, and Darcy torn between admiration and doubt.

Chapter 8

Summary

Jane's bad cold worsens and Elizabeth realises that only Bingley is sincere in his anxiety for her sister. Behind her back, Elizabeth is very unkindly criticised by Miss Bingley, but neither Bingley nor Darcy can be brought to join in the criticism. After dinner, when Jane is asleep, Elizabeth reluctantly joins her hosts in the drawing room, and Miss Bingley seeks to expose Elizabeth's deficiencies by turning the conversation to the topic of a woman's accomplishments. This she does to impress Darcy, but Darcy's comments, if applied to Elizabeth, are complimentary, rather than censorious. The chapter deepens our understanding of the characters of the Netherfield household.

Commentary

Throughout, Elizabeth's spontaneity is contrasted with the artificial sophistication of Bingley's sisters, more especially Caroline Bingley. The sisters do nothing natural, are always playing a game and are conscious of nothing except the *effect* they wish to make. Their concern for Jane ceases the minute they close the bedroom door on her; their abuse of Elizabeth begins the second she leaves the room. It is significant that they think Elizabeth, among her other shortcomings, has 'no style'. Caroline Bingley, always seeking to degrade Elizabeth in Darcy's eyes, refers to the Bennet's 'low connections'. Bingley, all heart, considers such connections irrelevant; but Darcy, whose head governs his heart, recognises that they must 'materially lessen' the Bennet sisters' chances of marrying well. In discussing the 'idea of an accomplished woman', Elizabeth satirically wonders at Darcy's knowing anyone able to live up to his very high expectations – to the annoyance of Miss Bingley, who imagines she herself qualifies. Darcy, gravely speaking of improving the mind through reading, obliquely compliments Elizabeth, who is, like himself, fond of books; once Elizabeth leaves them, Miss Bingley accuses her of employing the 'mean art' of winning the approval of men by undervaluing women. Loyal to Elizabeth in her absence, and angered by Miss Bingley's all too obvious arts, Darcy retorts that 'there is meanness in *all* the arts which ladies sometimes condescend to employ for captivation'.

Chapter 9

Summary

Since Jane continues to be ill, a note is sent to her mother, who is only too happy to visit Netherfield, accompanied by Charlotte and Lydia. Mrs Bennet is in much less of a hurry to arrange for Jane to return home. Predictably, she misunderstands Darcy's remark that there is less variety of people in the country than in the town, and embarrassingly tries to triumph over him by boasting that society in Meryton and its neighbourhood is equal to any other. Elizabeth tries desperately to suppress her mother's indiscretions, but not very successfully. Before returning to Longbourn with her mother, Lydia has the temerity to ask Bingley if he will keep his promise of giving a ball, and is assured it shall take place once Jane is better.

Commentary

Throughout, Elizabeth is aware of how the vulgarity of her mother and the forwardness of her silly sisters must be judged by the highly critical company at Netherfield: she trembles 'lest her mother should be exposing herself again'. Her own proper pride is threatened, and she resents Darcy's patronising forbearance. There is a real point in the brief discussion about character. Bingley is aware of his own impulsiveness and admits he would be capable of leaving Netherfield 'in five minutes'. Elizabeth claims to understand Bingley 'perfectly' and he regrets he is 'so easily seen through'. She denies that 'a deep, intricate character' is necessarily preferable to his own, which by implication is superficial and straightforward, and it is just possible this denial is made with Darcy in mind, since he has not her approval, though his character is deep and intricate. Elizabeth's preference for more complex characters is justified in terms of the *amusement* they afford, and we might recall that she found, or pretended to find, her first encounter with Darcy amusing. It is also worth noting that Bingley will later put into practice his claim that he could abruptly leave Netherfield.

Chapter 10

Summary

Jane begins to improve. In the evening, Darcy writes letters, interrupted by Miss Bingley. Darcy is much more irritated than flattered by the interruptions, and Elizabeth, sitting nearby with her needlework, is greatly entertained. Bingley and Darcy exchange criticisms of one another, first in respect of their styles in letter-writing, then in respect of their characters. Elizabeth tends to side with Bingley. Mrs Hurst and Miss Bingley entertain the company with songs, during which Elizabeth is puzzled by the way in which Darcy fixes his eyes on her. When asked by Darcy to dance, she refuses. Afterwards, Miss Bingley, aware of Darcy's growing liking for Elizabeth, spitefully taunts Darcy with talk about Elizabeth's socially inferior relations. When, next day, Darcy and Miss Bingley meet Mrs Hurst and Elizabeth walking in the garden, Mrs Hurst links Darcy's free arm, leaving Elizabeth to walk behind, since the path is too narrow to permit more than three to walk abreast. Darcy therefore suggests they all walk in the broader avenue, but Elizabeth escapes, happy to be free of their company.

Commentary

We share Elizabeth's amusement at Miss Bingley's officious display of affection, and enjoy Darcy's snub when he asks leave to defer the 'raptures' she wishes him to write on her behalf to his sister. When Bingley jibes that Darcy 'studies too much for words of four syllables', we remember that he has no enthusiasm for books and is at that moment playing cards with the philistine Mr Hurst. Darcy shrewdly perceives that Bingley's claim to carelessness, as a letter-writer and as a man, is 'an indirect boast'. He puts his finger on a lack of firmness in Bingley's character and defeats Elizabeth's attempts to interpret what he says as a compliment, since Bingley, he insists, is too obliging, even when there is no rational basis for him to be so. Bingley banters, with some edge to his accusation, that Darcy is intimidatingly severe, and Elizabeth checks her laugh at Darcy's expense because she perceives he is rather offended. This is the first time in the novel her sympathy is aroused for Darcy, however briefly. When he watches her while there is music, she is so far from any suspicion that he has any regard for her that she imagines there must be something wrong about her appearance or manner, and she is wholly counter-suggestive to his proposal to dance, convincing herself he is scheming some means whereby he can *despise* her. We remember how he did just that at their first encounter and cannot but suspect that on that occasion she was more deeply hurt than her making fun of it suggested. Her prejudice precludes her drawing the obvious conclusions from the attentions Darcy pays her, and his sensitiveness in suggesting the avenue walk fails to register with her.

Chapter 11

Summary
Jane is improving. She comes down to the drawing room and, after congratulations from everyone on her recovery, sits by the fireside, where she
is joined by Bingley, to Elizabeth's satisfaction. After tea, Miss Bingley
tries to impress Darcy by sitting nearby and reading, but quickly tires of
this and invites Elizabeth to walk up and down the room with her. Her
civility to Elizabeth attracts Darcy's attention. He declines to join them in
their indoor walk, and Miss Bingley and Elizabeth both banter with him,
though Miss Bingley quickly gets left out, especially when the sensitive
topic of pride is discussed, and soon proposes they should have a little
music.

Commentary
We should note that Bingley's sisters do have accomplishments: they can
speak well and entertainingly and exercise their wit when discussing people
they know. But this sophistication is hardly apparent in Miss Bingley's
pathetically naïve flattery of Darcy, as when she chooses the second volume
of the book he is reading, or very *un*subtly declares that in her house she
would be miserable without 'an excellent library' (with Pemberley clearly
in mind), or expresses a preference for conversation, rather than dancing.
Elizabeth's calculated teasing of Darcy is, in fact, much more sophisticated.
She takes up Miss Bingley's suggestion that Darcy is not to be laughed at,
only to confess she dearly loves a laugh. The negative implications of this
are unspoken. She quickly counters Darcy's moral objection by morally
affirming that she never ridicules 'what is wise and good'. Again there are
unspoken negative implications, and Elizabeth comes very near the bone
when she counters his claim that he tries to avoid 'weaknesses which often
expose a strong understanding to ridicule' by answering: 'Such as vanity
and pride'. Conscious of Elizabeth's sarcasm, Darcy attempts to distinguish
between vanity, which is never justifiable, and a proper pride, which is. He
gravely confesses to his shortcomings, but Elizabeth, prejudiced as usual, is
more concerned with repartee than with listening seriously to him. The
chapter shows us that Miss Bingley's palpable designs on Darcy meet with
constant rebuffs: he not only fails to respond, but takes a punitive satisfaction in *not* responding to her. On the other hand, he is always aware of
Elizabeth, who gives him no encouragement whatever, and is always
willing to engage in conversation with her, even though their exchanges
have edge.

Chapter 12

Summary

Elizabeth writes to her mother, asking for the carriage to bring Jane and herself home. Mrs Bennet wishes to prolong Jane's stay and cannot agree to help for some time. Pressed by Elizabeth, Jane approaches Bingley and his carriage is promised for the next day, when the sisters' departure is felt as a relief by Miss Bingley and Darcy.

Commentary

Miss Bingley's civility towards Elizabeth is in proportion to Elizabeth's distancing herself from Darcy. She sees what Elizabeth, departing 'in the liveliest spirits', is blind to – that Darcy is captivated by her. With typical severity, Darcy is hard on himself, burying his head in a book to avoid the temptation to look at Elizabeth; but note, too, that his relief at Elizabeth's departure comes in part from the sympathy he feels for her because of the uncivil treatment she receives at Miss Bingley's hands. It is ironic that Miss Bingley's attempts to degrade Elizabeth achieve a wholly opposite effect. The return of the sisters to Longbourn displeases Mrs Bennet, but pleases her husband, whose need for sensible company cannot be met during their absence.

Chapter 13

Summary

The following day brings a letter from Mr Collins, a cousin of Mr Bennet's, though he is unknown to the family, except as the man who will inherit Longbourn when Mr Bennet dies. He has recently taken holy orders and, under the patronage of Lady Catherine de Bourgh, has been made rector of Hunsford. After announcing his wish to be on good terms with the Bennets, he invites himself to Longbourn for a week, and duly arrives, disarming Mrs Bennet's hostility with assurances that he has come prepared to admire her daughters.

Commentary

The reception given to Mr Collins's letter by various members of the family is very revealing of character. Mrs Bennet's conviction that Collins is 'odious', because he will inherit their house, is reversed by the hope that he may be marriageable. Jane is slow on the uptake, but finds something good to say of him. Mary, intellectually pretentious herself, fails to recognise the pomposity of the letter's style, while to Catherine and Lydia, interested only in officers, a clergyman has no significance whatever. It is

Elizabeth who at once sees through the letter to the man: 'Can he be a sensible man, sir?' Typically, her father has 'great hopes of finding him quite the reverse'. When Mr Collins arrives, he is exactly the oddity Mr Bennet hopes for, pompous, sycophantic, all admiration for the girls, which pleases Mrs Bennet, but also, less pleasingly, all admiration for the house he will inherit.

Chapter 14

Summary

After dinner, Collins speaks at solemn length about his patroness, Lady Catherine de Bourgh, and Mr Bennet is not slow to egg him on, for his own and Elizabeth's amusement. After tea, Collins reads to the family from a book of sermons, but is rudely interrupted by Lydia's chatter, and is 'much offended'. At Collins's request, Mr Bennet takes him to the card table for a game of backgammon.

Commentary

The character of Collins is exposed by Mr Bennet, who leads him by the nose in conversation and delightedly shows him to be the ass he is. Collins's grovelling adulation and servile flattery of Lady Catherine should not deceive us into imagining that he is deficient in self-importance. He takes offence at Lydia's interruption and his assurances that he bears her 'no ill will' are a testimony to his actually doing so. Briefly, he is very much aware of the social hierarchy and wishes to exact from those he thinks his inferiors all the deference he bestows on his superiors.

Chapter 15

Summary

Collins's magnanimous plan of making amends for his future inheritance by marrying one of the Bennet sisters leads to his first thinking of Jane, on the grounds of seniority, but Mrs Bennet diverts his regard to Elizabeth, who has no suitor. Encouraged by Mr Bennet, who begins to find him too much of a good thing, Collins joins the sisters in their walk to Meryton. There they meet for the first time Wickham, a newcomer to the regiment, who makes a highly favourable impression on everyone by the charm of his appearance and manner. While they talk in the streets, Bingley and Darcy, on horseback, approach to pay their respects. Elizabeth is surprised and puzzled by the agitated manner in which Darcy and Wickham behave when they unexpectedly find themselves in one another's company. The

20

Bennet sisters, accompanied by Collins, call on their aunt, Mrs Philips, who invites them to dine with her the next day.

Commentary
Further evidence of Collins's fatuousness and incongruous mixture of 'self-importance and humility' is provided by the way in which he switches his romantic interest from Jane to Elizabeth in the time it takes Mrs Bennet to poke the fire, and overwhelms Mrs Philips with 'an excess of good breeding'. It should not be forgotten that the novel developed from an earlier story entitled *First Impressions*, and the impression Wickham first makes is that of a model romantic hero; but the alert reader, aware of the recurrent theme of reality and appearance, will note that the word 'appearance' is repeatedly used in respect of Wickham: he is 'of most gentlemanlike appearance'; everyone is struck by his 'air'; his 'appearance' is said to be 'greatly in his favour'. Darcy still struggles with himself to resist Elizabeth by not looking at her, but she of all the company is quick to see the effect of the meeting between Wickham and Darcy. She longs to know the meaning of it – an indication that she is far from indifferent in her feelings about Darcy, even if the feelings are hostile.

Chapter 16

Summary
The Bennet sisters, with Collins, dine with their aunt and uncle, and Wickham is among the officers who join the party. Elizabeth is delighted when he chooses to sit near her, and when he raises Darcy as a topic of conversation, she encourages him to talk. Wickham is the son of Darcy's father's steward. Darcy's father, to whom he was a favourite, had provided for Wickham to become a clergyman and take 'a most valuable living', but Darcy himself is said to have dishonourably withheld the living, largely out of jealousy. Picking up Lady Catherine de Bourgh's name from Collins, who never tires of celebrating his patroness, Wickham tells Elizabeth that Lady Catherine is a fitting aunt for Darcy, being arrogant and offensively proud. When he goes on to say that it is believed Darcy will marry her daughter, Elizabeth remembers Miss Bingley's desperate efforts to secure Darcy and smiles to herself.

Commentary
Wickham's story is fairly subtly told. He feels his way forward in telling it, and his malice is calculated in proportion to the encouragement Elizabeth gives him. Moreover, he is careful not to overdo his condemnation: Darcy is allowed to have *some* merit from family, filial and brotherly pride, and

is said to be honourable with his rich friends, though unjust to the less prosperous. We are given a subtle exposition of Elizabeth's feelings, which are more complex than might appear at a first glance. What she 'chiefly wished to hear' from Wickham is an account of Darcy. She might legitimately claim that she is entitled to feel some satisfaction in hearing something detrimental to Darcy, but the indications are that she has a very much more than ordinary concern about him. Why should she be so very eager to hear Darcy spoken ill of? She shows some vestiges of her usual good sense, asking what Darcy's motive could possibly be and expressing wonder that his pride does not keep him from dishonesty, but in general her critical intelligence gives way to naïve prejudice. Taken in by Wickham's superficial gentlemanliness, she never asks herself whether any gentleman would speak in this way on a first meeting with a young lady; she responds to his play for pity – 'I have been a disappointed man' – and to his facile sentiments – 'Till I can forget his father, I can never defy or expose *him*' – with a generous heart, but not much common sense, even though she knows that she 'had not thought so very ill' of Darcy previously. When Elizabeth honours Wickham for his sentiments and thinks him 'handsomer than ever' as he expresses them, we should ask *why*. We know perfectly well that Darcy feels Elizabeth's captivation, but has explicit reasons against it, and therefore seeks to escape from it. Elizabeth has statable reasons against Darcy, too, and it may be she is also escaping from something in herself. There is an ambivalence in her preoccupation with Darcy and it is arguable that by so readily believing the worst about him she is escaping from self-knowledge and is *protecting* herself against ambiguous feelings that she cannot risk coming to terms with. We know she was deeply hurt by Darcy's pride during their first encounter. One outcome of this would be for her to make herself invulnerable to any further injury of the kind, and this she might do by convincing herself that Darcy is a sham, with no true grounds for pride.

Chapter 17

Summary

Elizabeth takes Jane into her confidence, giving her an account of Wickham's story. Jane, typically, wishing to believe well of both Darcy and Wickham, believes there must be some misunderstanding and professes not to know what to think, while Elizabeth 'knows exactly what to think'. Bingley and his sisters call at Longbourn with invitations to a ball at Netherfield, the prospect of which raises hopes in all the Bennet sisters.

Collins dampens Elizabeth's enthusiasm by claiming the first two dances with her, and her mother leaves her in no doubt that he is her suitor.

Commentary

In knowing 'exactly what to think' of Darcy, Elizabeth exercises, for once, poorer judgement than Jane, who pertinently asks: 'Can his most intimate friends be so excessively deceived in him? Oh! no.' Elizabeth looks forward to dancing with Wickham, but significantly the pleasure of this consists as much in seeing Darcy's discomfiture as in being partner to 'a young man of such amiable appearance' (again the key word 'appearance' occurs). Meanwhile, Elizabeth is brought to face the fact that Collins has marked her out to be his wife. Nothing could be better timed to make her well disposed towards the apparently romantic Wickham than the advances of so grotesque a suitor.

Chapter 18

Summary

Wickham does not attend the ball at Netherfield and Elizabeth, disappointed, suspects Darcy has prevailed on Bingley not to invite him. Her dances with Collins are a torture to her, but later Darcy asks her to dance and she accepts, too surprised to know what she is doing. As they dance, Elizabeth banters with Darcy, then turns their talk to Wickham. Darcy freezes her out. They are approached by Sir William Lucas, who draws Darcy's unwelcome attention to Bingley and Jane, hinting without subtlety at their marriage. Resuming their talk, Elizabeth insinuates her suspicions about Darcy, who defensively suggests that she is 'blinded by prejudice'. When he leaves her, Elizabeth is approached by Miss Bingley, who warns her against Wickham; however, Elizabeth refuses to believe anything from that source. Nor will she take Jane's word when she tells her that Bingley has assured her that Wickham has deserved to lose Darcy's regard. Collins, having discovered that Darcy is present, rejects Elizabeth's advice not to introduce himself to Darcy and is deservedly snubbed in consequence, though he is too thick-skinned to realise it. This, Elizabeth feels, is shaming, since Collins is her cousin; but worse follows. Darcy is placed sufficiently close to Mrs Bennet to hear her boast openly of Jane's being soon married to Bingley; Mary Bennet gives an embarrassing musical performance and finally her scheming mother ensures that they are the last family to leave.

Commentary

Elizabeth's prejudice is well aired in this chapter. She rejects all evidence in favour of Darcy as 'blind partiality' and resists any suggestion that he may be 'agreeable' by expressing her determination to hate him. This may in itself indicate that she is half conscious of her need to avoid analysing her feelings for Darcy; her psychological security depends on his being as she is 'determined' to think of him – proud and bad. Her repeated references to Darcy's self-confessed tendency to 'resentment' are directed at establishing *his* guilt, so justifying *her* prejudice. But she has a highly developed sense of *pride*, as well as prejudice; indeed, the two are intimately connected. Her prejudice towards Darcy has its origin in hurt pride, and she is too proud to accept Miss Bingley's warning, which to some extent may be kindly meant, even if it is gratuitously snobbish. There is more than a grain of truth in her mocking assertion that she and Darcy have 'a great similarity' in the turn of their minds, and a proper self-respect is very evident in both of them. Elizabeth feels ashamed of her mother's boasting, Mary's unjustifiable display of inferior talent, her cousin Collins's foolish disregard for 'good form' because these are members of her family and she feels degraded and diminished by their insensitiveness. But by what standards does she judge them? Surely, by the standards she shares with Darcy himself, however much her prejudice may seek to deny it. When she mockingly declares that she and Darcy have 'a great similarity' in the turn of their minds, it is as if she is trying to block out a deeper truth with light-hearted banter.

Chapter 19

Summary

Abetted by Mrs Bennet, Collins gets Elizabeth alone and makes his proposal of marriage, formally stating reasons for it. As a clergyman, he wishes to set an example to his flock; he wishes, further, to add to his happiness; and no less importantly, he has received Lady Catherine de Bourgh's autocratic encouragement to marry. His altruism also leads him to do a favour to the Bennets by marrying one of the daughters. Having given his reasons, he assures Elizabeth of the violence of his affection. She politely declines his proposal. He refuses to believe she is sincere, promises to renew his proposal and again dismisses Elizabeth's very direct refusal, confident that no one with so small a fortune could afford to turn down so advantageous an offer. Her protestations that she is not playing the role of 'an elegant female', but is behaving like 'a rational creature' are ignored. He tells her he will prevail by enlisting her parents' authority.

Commentary

This is one of the most memorable proposals of marriage ever made and is a model of comic wit. It is made credible because at the time marriage, as Charlotte Lucas claims, was 'the only honourable provision' (Chapter 22) for a young woman without means: a point taken very much to heart by Collins. The chapter is almost entirely a dialogue, which gives it an appropriately theatrical quality. Collins, conceitedly advancing his 'reasons' before he is 'run away with' by his feelings, is more grotesque than ever. He has just enough perception to recognise that Elizabeth has 'wit and vivacity', but hopes that by bringing her as a wife into the presence of Lady Catherine (for him, the ultimate felicity), these qualities will be 'tempered with. . .silence and respect'. What he is actually offering her is self-annihilation! This she well understands, but is helpless to make *him* understand, so that the chapter ends in the cross-purposes Elizabeth has desperately struggled to avoid throughout. That she should at this time have met the romantic Wickham and in part surrended to his charm adds a further ironic dimension to this scene.

Chapter 20

Summary

Mrs Bennet hears of Elizabeth's refusal with consternation and alarms Collins by incautiously calling Elizabeth headstrong and foolish. She bursts into the library, demanding that Mr Bennet use a father's authority to bring Elizabeth to an acceptance, and Elizabeth is sent for. He places before her what he playfully calls 'an unhappy alternative': that her mother will never see her again if she does not marry Collins, while he will never see her again if she does. Elizabeth is relieved, but continues to be harassed by her mother. When Charlotte Lucas visits Longbourn, she is excitedly told of Elizabeth's recalcitrance, and her curiosity is aroused about Collins, whose pride is hurt.

Commentary

Mr Bennet, as ever, shows a 'calm unconcern' in the face of his wife's extreme agitation and playfully sides with Elizabeth, his favourite. Mrs Bennet wants Elizabeth 'brought to reason', but as Elizabeth noted from the start, Collins is not a sensible man, and it is entirely *reasonable* for her to reject him. The slightest hint of a solution to Collins's problem in finding a wife is given when we are told that he arouses Charlotte Lucas's curiosity.

Chapter 21

Summary

Charlotte Lucas shows herself understanding to Collins and his hurt pride. While in Meryton, Elizabeth renews her acquaintance with Wickham, who explains his absence from the ball was self-imposed, since he wished to avoid any possible unpleasantness arising between himself and Darcy. He continues to pay Elizabeth particular attention and she introduces him to her parents when he walks her home. Presently, Jane receives a letter from Miss Bingley. It is a bombshell and explains how her brother went on business to London and has been joined there by everyone else from Netherfield, to which they have no immediate intention of returning. Bingley himself is said to be attracted to Darcy's sister. Elizabeth is quick to detect Caroline Bingley's motives in writing – her snobbishness and hope that if her brother marries Darcy's sister, she may stand a better chance of marrying Darcy; but Jane thinks too well of her 'friend' to agree, though she shares some of Elizabeth's faith that Bingley loves her. Both sisters keep the letter and its contents from their mother.

Commentary

Wickham's explanation of his absence from the ball is at variance with the claim he makes in Chapter 16, where he insists: 'it is not for *me* to be driven away by Mr Darcy. If *he* wishes to avoid seeing *me*, he must go.' This seems to escape Elizabeth's notice altogether, and her growing regard for Wickham is obvious from her introducing him to her parents. It is probable that her loyalty to him has been increased by the warnings she has had against him, and her determination to think ill of Darcy logically requires her to think correspondingly well of Wickham. Yet her good sense, where she is not emotionally involved, is enough to see clear through Caroline Bingley. As she wittily observes, if Darcy had shown Miss Bingley half the affection Bingley has shown Jane, 'she would have ordered her wedding clothes'. But her judgement of Bingley is wrong. He is more easily influenced than she imagines, and he will not quickly return to Netherfield. Jane's charity in reading Miss Bingley's letter – 'she means (most kindly) to put me on my guard' – is matched by a cruelty on Miss Bingley's part that is so excessive as to be slightly out of character. The general reference to Jane's 'beaux' is unkind, and the hope she expresses of Bingley's marrying Georgina Darcy is pointedly unkind; but in expressing her belief that 'a sister's partiality' is not misleading her when she calls her brother 'most capable of engaging any woman's heart', she is quite gratuitously turning the knife in the wound.

Chapter 22

Summary

Charlotte Lucas's attentions to Collins are not disinterested, and he rises to the bait, proposing marriage. Her scheming has secured 'the only honourable provision' for someone in her position, and despite her total lack of illusions about Collins, she claims to be content. Collins leaves Longbourn next day, having at Charlotte's request kept their engagement secret, but promising a speedy return, to the dismay of Mr Bennet. Mrs Bennet now entertains hopes that Mary might be married off to Collins, but Charlotte Lucas comes the following day to tell Elizabeth of her engagement. Elizabeth cannot wholly conceal her horror, while Charlotte defends her decision with the logic of a realist.

Commentary

The author enjoys herself at the expense of Collins, speaking of 'the fire and independence of his character' and presenting us with the ludicrous spectacle of his slyly hastening from Longbourn to Lucas Lodge, 'to throw himself at [Charlotte's] feet'. Charlotte meets him half way, literally and metaphorically, from desire; but far from being romantic desire, it is from 'the pure and disinterested desire of an establishment', i.e. desire of the material security of a home. By using 'pure' and 'disinterested' here, when the precisely *opposite* sense is intended, Jane Austen ensures that Charlotte also is satirised. More intelligent than Collins, Charlotte knows him to be foolish and disagreeable; she also knows how Elizabeth is likely to respond to her news, and has the grace to give way to 'a momentary confusion', though she generally keeps 'a steady countenance' and resolutely asserts she is an unromantic realist. It is clear that Elizabeth has never taken seriously enough the cynicism towards marriage expressed by Charlotte in Chapter 6. In consequence, Charlotte, who can so cold-bloodedly sacrifice 'every better feeling to wordly advantage', loses some of Elizabeth's good opinion.

Chapter 23

Summary

Sir William Lucas announces to the Bennet family at large what only Elizabeth knows in confidence: that his daughter is to marry Collins. Elizabeth tries to rescue him with congratulations from the embarrassment of her family's incredulity. Lady Lucas triumphs over Mrs Bennet by having a daughter who is to marry the inheritor of Longbourn and Mrs

Bennet's limited good nature is painfully stretched when Collins writes to say he will soon visit them again, which he does. Meanwhile, Miss Bingley has not replied to a letter Jane has sent her, and Mrs Bennet's distress is added to by the rumour that Bingley will not return to Netherfield during the winter. Elizabeth suspects that Bingley is being kept away by the united efforts of his sisters and Darcy.

Commentary
The Bennet fortunes are at a low ebb. The shattering news of Charlotte's engagement to Collins is greeted with such disbelief and rudeness that it takes all Sir William's 'courtliness' and 'good breeding' to carry off his announcement. It is worth noting that Mr Bennet is grateful at finding the sensible Charlotte 'as foolish as his wife, and more foolish than his daughter', since his judgements, if not his actions, tend to be sound. Elizabeth still cannot convince herself that Bingley does not love Jane; she feeds her prejudice, with some justice, by blaming Darcy and Bingley's sisters for his failure to return.

Chapter 24

Summary
Miss Bingley's letter confirms the rumour that Bingley will not return to Netherfield and labours his attachment to Miss Darcy. Jane stoically accepts her position, believing well of everyone and concluding that she has been more deceived by her own vanity than by Bingley. Elizabeth persists in thinking Bingley loves Jane, continues to resent those who influence him, and is angry that he should be so weak as to allow himself to be manipulated by them. She is disillusioned with Charlotte Lucas and the more she sees of life, the more she dislikes what she sees – inconstancy, lack of integrity and principle. Mrs Bennet feels that Jane has been abused, and Mr Bennet cannot therefore resist advancing arguments in favour of being jilted. The one bright spot in all this is that Wickham is a frequent visitor. He has now publicly exposed Darcy's dishonourable conduct, and Meryton society is delighted to have its prejudice confirmed.

Commentary
By believing Bingley to be 'the slave of his designing friends', Elizabeth continues to shift some of the blame for his treatment of Jane on to her enemies, though she is forced to admit that Bingley lacks 'proper resolution'. Her judgement on matters relating to Bingley and his circle is reasonable and in essence sound, so it follows that Jane's angelic disposition

28

towards Bingley's sisters and Darcy is misplaced; but Jane does show a strength of judgement superior to Elizabeth's when she asserts that if Bingley were truly attached to her, his sisters and friend 'could not succeed'. The distinction drawn by Elizabeth between 'happiness' and 'wealth and consequence' helps to explain both her condemnation of those who manipulate Bingley and her disappointment over Charlotte Lucas. As usual, Elizabeth's repartee with her father is entertaining, but behind his detachment, which allows him to turn Jane's disaster into a jest, there is a very clear indication that he has taken Wickham's measure. But what could be a warning is lost on Elizabeth, whose concentration is taken up with matching her father's wit with an equally clever reply about 'Jane's good fortune'. It is highly significant that Wickham has waited until Darcy is in London before levelling accusations against him. Elizabeth's prejudice in Wickham's favour is apparently so strong as to block out all recollection of his telling her (Chapter 16): 'Till I can forget his father, I can never defy or expose *him*.'

Chapter 25

Summary

Collins returns home for Christmas, which brings Mrs Bennet's brother, Mr Gardiner, and his wife to Longbourn. The Gardiners are favourites with Elizabeth, who confides in her aunt, telling her about Jane's unhappiness. Mrs Gardiner proposes that Jane should visit her in London. Elizabeth, severely critical of those responsible for separating Bingley from Jane, agrees that a change of scene will be good for her sister; and she predicts that, since the Gardiners live in an unfashionable part of the city, Jane will be safe from the attentions of Bingley's snobbish sisters and Darcy. Mrs Gardiner notices that Elizabeth and Wickham are rather more intimate than she thinks wise.

Commentary

The Gardiners, so much liked by Elizabeth, are very much more to the credit of her family than her mother, her younger sisters and Mr and Mrs Philips: their judgements are grounded in good sense and a proper sense of values. Mrs Gardiner's proposal that Jane should stay with her in London is practical, sensible, and made *without* laying blame on Bingley. Mrs Bennet's fatuousness – her self-pity, petty rivalry, equal gratitude for her relations and fashionable long sleeves – is the more apparent when she is set next to Mrs Gardiner. But through Mrs Gardiner we are made to look more closely at Elizabeth, too. Mrs Gardiner will not let her neice get away with vague talk of violent love: she is older, much more a woman of the world than Elizabeth, and aware that young men often exaggerate what they profess to feel for young women. She knows Jane's nature, and Elizabeth's too, which could have withstood being jilted, by laughter (a faint echo of Elizabeth's first encounter with Darcy). Elizabeth's sense of the injustice done to Jane is expressed with intense bitterness and irony and has Darcy as its focus. He has 'custody' of Bingley and would think 'a month's ablution' too little, if he himself were to enter the unfashionable area of London where the Gardiners live. The intensity of Elizabeth's feelings against Darcy might have alerted her aunt, were it not for Elizabeth's open preference for Wickham; but it is significant that Mrs Gardiner, with such obvious practical sense, thinks Elizabeth should be warned against this connection.

Chapter 26

Summary
Mrs Gardiner advises Elizabeth against an attachment with Wickham, and she agrees 'not to be in a hurry' in pursuing it. Collins comes to Lucas Lodge and fixes his wedding day, and before she leaves to be married Charlotte Lucas asks Elizabeth to correspond with her, and to visit her at Hunsford. Elizabeth agrees, though she is conscious that their friendship can never again be all that it once was. Jane, who is now staying with the Gardiners, visits Miss Bingley, who in belatedly returning her visit makes it clear from her manner that she cares nothing for Jane. Elizabeth is confirmed in her worst suspicions about Bingley, whom she blames for want of resolution, and his acquaintance. Wickham, meanwhile, cools his relationship with Elizabeth, turning his attentions to a Miss King, whose attraction is that she has come into a fortune. Elizabeth writes to give her aunt an account of this, and if she is not significantly hurt by Wickham, it is because she realises that, though responsive to his charm, she has never been truly in love with him.

Commentary
Even Jane's 'angelic' nature cannot conceal from her the coldness of Miss Bingley, and she abandons all hope of Bingley's seeking her out at her aunt's. Characteristically, she is inclined to pity, rather than to resent, Caroline Bingley: her letter is sad, puzzled, but hardly reproachful. Elizabeth, on the contrary, is far less charitable, resentfully wishing Bingley badly married, as a punishment. In matters relating to herself, however, Elizabeth is more impartial. She listens respectfully to her aunt's objections to

Wickham, which are based on prudence. Affection, Mrs Gardiner argues, is a fine thing, but only when found in association with a suitable fortune. By a stroke of irony, Wickham is deflected from his interest in Elizabeth precisely because of a suitable fortune; but even then, Elizabeth exempts him from blame, out of charitable prejudice. His case, after all, is identical with Charlotte Lucas's – both have set money above affection – but Elizabeth is 'less clear-sighted' about it. She prides herself on her wit and rationality, yet wholly fails to heed her father's witty warning about Wickham in Chapter 24 (she even tells her aunt her father is 'partial to Mr Wickham'), and irrationally applies double standards, rather than admit he has behaved improperly. Her grounds for knowing she is not in love with Wickham are revealing, for had she seriously cared about him, she argues she would 'detest his very name' and 'wish him all manner of evil'. She knows what real love would have involved, though she fails to see that she entertains in respect of her 'enemy', Darcy, the very feelings she describes.

Chapter 27

Summary
Elizabeth keeps her promise and visits Charlotte Collins in March, travelling with Sir William and Charlotte's sister, Maria. Their journey is broken by their staying overnight with the Gardiners in Gracechurch Street, where Jane is found to be outwardly well, but dejected in spirit. Elizabeth and her aunt discuss Wickham's transference of his attentions to Miss King, an act that Elizabeth defends. Before the party sets out for Hunsford, Mrs Gardiner delights Elizabeth by inviting her to join Mr Gardiner and herself on a holiday touring the Lake District.

Commentary
With Jane away, and Elizabeth going away for some weeks, Mr Bennet's satirical detachment, really a defence against the world, is badly shaken: he almost admits to feelings he takes care to keep at arm's length, and when we consider what company he will be left with, once his favourite daughter goes, we can sympathise with him. Elizabeth's farewell to Wickham is friendly; indeed, she is convinced that, married or single, 'he must always be her model of the amiable and pleasing'. For his part, Wickham shows her he still cares for her, but the 'solicitude' he shows is felt by the reader to be improper. He enjoys flirtation, and cannot let go. The marriage theme is explored again in Elizabeth's discussion of Wickham with her aunt, who criticises Wickham's indelicacy in switching his attentions so abruptly and for such mercenary reasons. Elizabeth objects that her aunt,

in condemning Wickham for marrying into money, is contradicting views she has previously stated, and that if Miss King does not object, no one else has the right to. Mrs Gardiner's mature insight is apparent in her reply. Money is for her a necessary consideration, but not the *only* consideration; and the fact that Miss King has no objection to Wickham's too obvious tactics 'does not justify *him*'. There is a note of weariness, of flagging spirit in Elizabeth's replies. She now claims to have 'a very poor opinion of young men', to be 'sick of them all', though this is said with Bingley's treatment of her sister in mind, too. The tour of the Lakes offers an escape from men and the possibility of spiritual renewal – 'fresh life and vigour'. But her spirits have not sunk so low as to rob her of her satirical impulse. In Jane Austen's lifetime, the Lakes became popular as a place of tourism, and Elizabeth is sarcastic at the expense of tourists who go there to indulge their romantic imaginations and return home with very vague and imperfect recollections of the beauties they claim to be unforgettable.

Chapter 28

Summary
Sir William, Maria and Elizabeth are given a warm welcome by Charlotte when they arrive at Hunsford parsonage. Collins has not changed. He makes a display of his house, as if to remind Elizabeth of what she has missed, and his wife manages to avoid the embarrassment of his pompous behaviour by pretending not to notice it. The parsonage stands on the edge of Rosings Park, Lady Catherine de Bourgh's estate, and the view of her house is a constant source of rapture to Collins. Charlotte has made a comfortable home for herself. Her marriage is satisfactory when her husband is not present! Next day, there is great agitation when Lady Catherine's daughter, Miss de Bourgh, stops in her carriage outside the house to invite them all to dine at Rosings.

Commentary
The marriage theme is pursued in the portrait of life in the parsonage. Charlotte has the material comfort and security she expected out of marriage, but not a whit more. She is deaf to the embarrassing speeches of her husband, whom she shuts out of her life psychologically, and physically, when possible. But she keeps up the *pretence* of a satisfactory marriage. She admits to Elizabeth that she encourages Collins to work in the garden, but keeps a straight face about her motives. She knows Lady Catherine to be an insufferable snob, who constantly imposes her will on Collins and herself, but with the same straight face speaks of her with respect as 'a

most attentive neighbour'. Elizabeth recognises that Charlotte has come to terms with her lot, and found some contentment in it, even if it means putting up with the rudeness of the sickly and cross Miss de Bourgh, who keeps her waiting out of doors. But Elizabeth is, of course, eager to pick fault with Miss de Bourgh. She has been prejudiced against both Lady Catherine and her daughter by Wickham, who has hardly exaggerated in his account of them; and she is spitefully happy when she finds Miss de Bourgh's appearance is reassuringly in sharp contrast to the claims made for her by Miss Bingley. She is therefore 'a very proper wife' for Darcy, towards whom Elizabeth is so actively hostile. The cameo of Charlotte and Collins paying respects to a young lady who rudely detains them at her carriage is enhanced by the comic extravagance of Sir William Lucas, who stands constantly bowing at the parsonage door, 'in earnest contemplation of the greatness before him'.

Chapter 29

Summary

Lady Catherine summons the company at Hunsford parsonage to Rosings, for dinner. She lives up to the expectations raised in Wickham's description of her, being haughty and autocratic and intent on asserting her own superiority by treating her company as inferiors. All this is accepted by everyone except Elizabeth, who refuses to be overawed and preserves her independence of spirit. Lady Catherine is a conversational bully, capable of asking outrageous questions about those she considers her inferiors, but Elizabeth evades her hostess by means of her superior wit.

Commentary

We are admitted here to the grandeur and ostentation of Rosings and its owner, but very entertainingly. Sir William, despite his pretentions, is 'completely awed', and his daughter 'frightened almost out of her senses'; Collins is, as ever, only too willing to play the role of sycophant and his wife to be seen and not heard; but if Elizabeth thinks Lady Catherine 'awful', it is in *our* sense of the word, not in the eighteenth-century sense. Lady Catherine does not inspire her with a sense of awe; indeed, Elizabeth can see no particular talent or merit in her that might claim her respect, and she will not be imposed on by mere 'money and rank'. She makes no apologies for the irregularities of her upbringing and dares to 'trifle' with her hostess. The author, too, satirises Lady Catherine, pointing out that 'nothing was beneath this great Lady's attention, which could furnish her with an occasion for dictating to others'. Amusingly, the party gather around Lady Catherine, before they leave, to hear her 'determine what weather they were to have tomorrow', as if she were God and good and bad weather lay in her gift.

Chapter 30

Summary

Sir William returns home at the end of a week. Additional insights are given into the routine of life at the parsonage and Rosings, from which come further dinner invitations. As Easter approaches, Darcy and his cousin, Colonel Fitzwilliam, come to stay at Rosings. When they visit the parsonage, Elizabeth asks Darcy whether he has seen Jane in London, deliberately embarrassing him.

Commentary

Elizabeth is quick to perceive that Charlotte's domestic arrangements are so ordered as to exclude her husband as much as possible. Charlotte, however, is quick to perceive what Elizabeth is blind to: that Darcy's visit is promptly made on her account. Although Darcy cannot resist the temptation to see Elizabeth, he continues to be haughty and taciturn. Colonel Fitzwilliam, who is pleasant in manner and easy in conversation, is an obvious foil to Darcy.

Chapter 31

Summary

Lady Catherine, having more important company, takes her time about sending an invitation to the parsonage, but eventually does so. Clearly, Colonel Fitzwilliam is attracted to Elizabeth: a fact that Lady Catherine resents and of which Darcy is immediately conscious. When Elizabeth plays the piano, Darcy stations himself to watch her, and there is repartee between them concerning their characters and their first encounter at the Meryton ball. It is significant that Elizabeth watches Darcy closely when Miss de Bourgh's merits are praised, but she fails to discern in him any symptom of concern.

Commentary

Elizabeth continues to be socially confident and is determined not to be intimidated by her surroundings, her hostess or Darcy. Lady Catherine's claim, that she herself would have excelled at music if only she had learnt it, splendidly demonstrates her self-important silliness, but her offer to Elizabeth of her housekeeper's piano is vulgar and insulting, and makes

Darcy blush for his aunt as Elizabeth has had to blush for her mother. The bantering between Elizabeth and Darcy is a sign of increasing intimacy, of something shared, even if there are critical undertones in what she says. Darcy, on the contrary, is steadily complimentary. His attentions are plain to the reader, but not to Elizabeth, who remains entrenched in her prejudice and fails to draw some obvious conclusions about his feelings for her.

Chapter 32

Summary
The following day, Darcy visits the parsonage and finds Elizabeth on her own. They talk guardedly about Bingley, Collins and Charlotte, and there is enough ambiguity in what is said for misunderstandings to arise. Presently Charlotte and her sister arrive and Darcy quickly leaves. Charlotte explains Darcy's visit by saying he must be in love with Elizabeth, but she is half talked out of the belief by Elizabeth. Darcy and Fitzwilliam continue to call at the parsonage, but even Charlotte cannot find sufficient evidence from his behaviour of Darcy's being in love with Elizabeth.

Commentary
There is great skill in the way the characters are shown to struggle in vain to make themselves understood and to understand one another, while all the clues necessary for a full understanding are given to the reader. Darcy is persistently misunderstood by Elizabeth. When he apologises for his intrusion, his politeness is misinterpreted as confusion at his being alone with someone he does not like; when he hints that she is superior to her surroundings at Longbourn (and is better fitted for Pemberley), she completely fails to take the hint. Though she admits Charlotte's 'excellent understanding', she wholly rejects Charlotte's shrewd suspicions. It is just possible that Elizabeth's satisfaction in being with the amiable Colonel Fitzwilliam is a way of protecting herself from facing up to the much stronger, though negative, feelings she has towards Darcy.

Chapter 33

Summary
Elizabeth is puzzled by Darcy's 'perverse' encounters with her. Though she recognises the attraction she has for Fitzwilliam and suspects, with some reason, that his confession that he cannot marry where he likes is meant for her, she remains as blind as ever to all clues as to what Darcy may feel. She learns that Fitzwilliam is joint guardian with Darcy of Miss Darcy, and

inadvertently startles him by asking whether she is 'difficult to manage'. When Bingley is mentioned, Fitzwilliam confirms Elizabeth's worst suspicions about Darcy, who has saved his friend from 'a most imprudent marriage'. Her resentment is acute, especially since she sees Darcy's interference as another instance of his snobbishness and pride.

Commentary

Elizabeth's misunderstanding of, and hostility towards Darcy is now as total as it can be. She cannot believe his encounters are deliberate and is herself perverse in supposing them perverse; but the worst evidence of all against Darcy is his part in separating Bingley from her sister Jane. She is sensitively aware of the shortcomings of her family, whether real or imagined, in Darcy's eyes, and now sees him as a monster of pride and the destroyer of 'the most generous heart in the world'. Why Fitzwilliam is startled by the reference to Miss Darcy becomes clear later, when we are let into the secret of her narrow escape from Wickham's designs.

Chapter 34

Summary

At the culminating point of Elizabeth's hostility against him (she is alone, feeding her anger by reading desolate letters from Jane), Darcy astonishes her by arriving with a proposal of marriage. The proposal is, however, flawed with misgivings he expresses about the social inferiority of her connections and by the honour he imagines he is conferring upon her. This angers Elizabeth, and his confident expectation of her acceptance provokes her into a hard-hitting rejection of him. For the first time, she honestly speaks her mind, accusing him of ruining both her sister's happiness and Wickham's career. She declares her long-standing dislike of him. He offers no apology and leaves her, ashamed, so he says, of the feelings he has had for her. She collapses in tears and confusedly admits that his loving her is gratifying, though any pity she feels is swamped by her lingering anger at his 'abominable pride'.

Commentary

What Darcy fails to understand is that Elizabeth has up to this point been moving *away* from him. His own growing affection has been so real for him that he cannot believe her to be unaware of it, just as she cannot believe he has failed to see her mounting antagonism towards him. Their accusations recapitulate the misunderstandings of the first half of the novel; then suddenly misunderstanding is over. From this point forward, their relationship will be one of deepening understanding of themselves and of each other. Elizabeth reads Jane's letters as if from a need to inflame her hatred of Darcy. She is, however negatively, deeply *involved* with him as she never has been with either Wickham or Fitzwilliam. Both of them turn pale with anger; each accuses the other of pride and, implicitly, of prejudice; each stubbornly refuses to make concessions to the other. She tells him he is unjust while he claims his feelings are just; and still more hurtfully, she accuses him of failing to behave in a 'gentleman-like manner', an accusation that is to rankle with him. Despite its profound importance, Darcy's condescending proposal has some superficial resemblances to Collins' earlier proposal. It is significant that Elizabeth says that within a month of knowing Darcy, she felt he was 'the last man in the world [she] could ever be prevailed upon to marry'. But no one was prevailing on her, and if the idea of marriage arose, even negatively, it could only have been in her mind!

Chapter 35

Summary

When Elizabeth is out walking the next day, Darcy appears and presents her with a letter. In it, he explains that, Jane and herself apart, her family is not one he considers suitable for Bingley to marry into; but more importantly, he claims he influenced Bingley against marrying Jane because she showed his friend no 'symptom of peculiar regard'. He offers no apology, except in so far as he may have misunderstood Jane's feelings for Bingley. Nor does he apologise for anything relating to Wickham, whom he exposes as dissolute, dishonourable and a liar. He tells of how Wickham took £3,000 in lieu of a clergyman's living, squandered the money, then asked for the living again. He even brings himself to reveal the near disgrace into which Wickham brought his sister by designing an elopement, and refers Elizabeth to Fitzwilliam for confirmation of all he says.

Commentary

The letter, temperately written, accepts some responsibility for Bingley, but with just the qualification that he is forgivable: Jane's modesty of behaviour was understandably thought by Darcy to have been *indifference*. We recall Charlotte's commenting (Chapter 6) that Jane must do more to help Bingley understand the truth of what she feels for him. Darcy's account of Wickham must inevitably bring Elizabeth to a realisation that she herself, not Darcy, has been unjust. Her mind has throughout been closed to whatever evidence ran counter to her prejudice. Two features of the letter indicate Darcy's continuing regard for Elizabeth: he reveals a painful family intimacy in absolute trust and signs off with tenderness.

Chapter 36

Summary
Though strongly prejudiced against him, Elizabeth reads and twice re-reads Darcy's letter. She comes, gradually and painfully, to acknowledge that she has been guilty of being 'blind, partial, prejudiced, absurd'. There is, she realises, more than a little truth in what is said about her family and about Jane's apparent indifference. The impropriety of Wickham's confiding in her at a first acquaintance suddenly strikes her, as do the inconsistencies in his story and behaviour. She returns, humiliated, to the parsonage and learns that Darcy and Fitzwilliam have paid their respects and left the neighbourhood.

Commentary
The letter forces Elizabeth to face up to some unpleasant home truths about her family, and still more humiliatingly about herself. The theme of appearance and reality is touched on: Wickham's air of having 'every virtue' is offset by Elizabeth's failure to recollect a single 'instance of goodness' in his behaviour, while Darcy's 'proud and repulsive' manners obscure a character that is never 'unprincipled or unjust'. And Elizabeth had prided herself on her cleverness and judgement! She can take a grain of comfort in Darcy's complimenting Jane and herself on transcending their family and background, but her eyes are open now, and she feels humiliation in coming to a new understanding of herself. This is the necessary condition for Elizabeth's emotional, intellectual and moral development, with which the second half of the novel is concerned.

Chapter 37

Summary
Lady Catherine renews her invitations to the parsonage, and is as officious as ever. It is the final week of Elizabeth's visit and she is depressed by coming more and more to realise that, though she still cannot approve Darcy, he has been just in criticising her family. Her father is irresponsible, her mother vulgar, her younger sisters 'ignorant, idle and vain'. Because of this, Jane has lost Bingley. Lady Catherine is right in detecting that Elizabeth is depressed in mood.

Commentary

Elizabeth re-reads Darcy's painful letter almost as if it were a love-letter, till she knows it by heart. The more she allows that he has justice on his side, the more she has to adjust her own views and feelings in a way that helps her to mature and to prepare her for future contact with Darcy. Her depression over her family is matched by Darcy's sorrow at leaving Rosings. He does the proper thing, but with a heavy heart.

Chapter 38

Summary

Before Elizabeth and Maria take their leave, Collins breakfasts with Elizabeth. He obliges her to express gratitude for the hospitality of his 'humble home', which she does, though she draws the line at praising Lady Catherine. He imagines he has an ideal marriage (reminding her of what she has lost by turning him down) and she feels compassion for Charlotte, married to such a man, even if she puts on a brave face. Elizabeth and Maria set out for Hertfordshire, interrupting their journey in London to visit the Gardiners and collect Jane.

Commentary

Charlotte has chosen marriage 'with her eyes open' and Elizabeth admires the way in which she makes the best of a bad job. Collins imagines that he and Charlotte are perfectly matched, when in fact Charlotte is alienated from him, and Elizabeth's compassion for her friend is aroused because her life with Collins can only grow worse with time. Elizabeth has not yet sorted herself out and cannot order her mind as to how much she should reveal to Jane of all that has happened.

Chapter 39

Summary

Elizabeth, Jane and Maria take leave of the Gardiners and are met on their journey home by Kitty and Lydia. Lydia has bought an ugly bonnet, wasting money given her to buy everyone lunch, and she talks excitedly of visiting Brighton, where the regiment stationed at Meryton are to camp for the summer. Wickham, moreover, is unattached, Miss King having gone to stay permanently in Liverpool. The younger sisters chatter vulgarly and Lydia jokes about how she would enjoy being the first of the sisters to marry. A warm welcome awaits Jane and Elizabeth at home.

Commentary

The chapter concentrates on the frivolity of Kitty and, in particular, Lydia, who is pushing, empty-headed and flirtatious. Her character is more fully realised here, in preparation for the important role she is to have when she elopes with Wickham, who is brought back into the story at this point, but not in a way that does him much credit. She reinforces the sense of shame Elizabeth feels for her family. Mr Bennet's welcome to Elizabeth has a simple sincerity, quite out of keeping with his usual contrived and witty manner of speaking.

Chapter 40

Summary

Elizabeth reveals to Jane Darcy's proposal and the contents of his letter, in so far as they concern Wickham; but she takes care to conceal whatever relates to Bingley. They resolve to keep what they know about Wickham to themselves. Mrs Bennet is melodramatically downcast: she has given up her expectations of seeing Jane and Elizabeth married and gloomily accepts she will lose her husband and be put out of her home by the Collinses.

Commentary

Characteristically, Jane wishes to believe well of *both* Darcy and Wickham. Though heart-broken, she still has consideration for the sufferings of others, including Darcy, whom Elizabeth begins to appreciate more the better she understands herself. The appearance and reality theme is neatly summarised when she says of Darcy and Wickham that 'one has all the goodness, and the other all the appearance of it'. Elizabeth comes more and more to see she has been 'vain and nonsensical', thinking herself 'uncommonly clever' and witty, when in fact she has been ignorant and unjust. The sisters' decision not to reveal what kind of man Wickham is profoundly affects new developments in the plot.

Chapter 41

Summary

To the desolation of Lydia and Kitty, the regiment moves to Brighton. They, and even their mother, wish to holiday there, but only Lydia goes, invited by the young wife of Colonel Foster. Kitty is extremely jealous. Elizabeth disapproves and asks her father to refuse Lydia permission, arguing that Lydia's improper behaviour reflects badly on the whole family. Mr Bennet refuses, denying that the family reputation can be at all damaged by Lydia. Wickham is to follow the regiment and takes his leave. Elizabeth despises his renewed attentions and lets him know that she has come to a better understanding of Darcy and of him. He is embarrassed but suggests that Darcy is honest only in appearance. When they part, it is with 'a mutual desire of never meeting again'.

Commentary

When Elizabeth tries to get her father to discipline Lydia, it is clear that Darcy's standards have become her own. She is more serious than she was and cannot simply treat her family's failings as a source of amusement, as her father does. He evades responsibility by treating the whole matter as a subject for irony, as when he suggests that Lydia can make a fool of herself with 'little expense or inconvenience to the family'. It is the witty but easy way out to pretend that the silly sisters will be a foil to enhance the good qualities of the two oldest. Wickham's insensitiveness is apparent from his renewing his attentions to Elizabeth. She has the moral courage to indicate her better appreciation of Darcy, and his accusation that Darcy has only the *appearance* of honesty is a staggering and ironic piece of effrontery.

Chapter 42

Summary

Elizabeth examines the ill-judged marriage of her parents and reflects on the ill effects it has had on the entire family. She clings to the thought of her trip to the Lake District, but when eventually she leaves with the Gardiners, it has to be restricted to Derbyshire. Elizabeth is alarmed by her aunt's wish to look over Pemberley, Darcy's home, and reconciles herself to it only after she is assured that Darcy himself is absent.

Commentary

Though a favourite, Elizabeth is not blind to her father's failings. As a husband, he amuses himself by teasing a wife he holds in contempt; as a father, he prefers to be indulgent because it takes too much effort to act responsibly. His error was to marry a stupid and vulgar woman because she was pretty. Thereafter, he cuts himself off from her. Charlotte similarly makes a mistake. She marries for material security, and cuts herself off from Collins. Marriage based on physical attraction alone, or contracted simply for security, is shown to be highly unsatisfactory. But attraction and security *together* make for a good marriage, as the Gardiners show. In coming to terms with herself, Elizabeth has been moving closer to Darcy's standards and attitudes; but it is obvious that she is now drawing physically closer to him, too.

Chapter 43

Summary

Elizabeth and her aunt and uncle discover the delights of Pemberley and hear Darcy's praises sung by the old housekeeper. In her testimony, Darcy has had a good nature from childhood: he is a generous employer and landlord, kind in his personal relationships and an ideal brother. Wickham, on the other hand, has not the housekeeper's respect and is said to have 'turned out very wild'. To the embarrassment of both, Elizabeth and Darcy (who has returned to Pemberley earlier than expected) meet in the grounds, and part after a brief but polite exchange of greetings. Elizabeth is impressed by how much he has improved. She resumes her walk with her aunt and uncle only to find Darcy approaching again. Contrary to her expectations, he is politely friendly to the Gardiners, who discreetly draw the conclusion that Darcy and their niece are better known to each other than Elizabeth has admitted. Their belief is strongly confirmed when Darcy expresses the wish to introduce his sister, Georgiana, to Elizabeth.

Commentary

Elizabeth cannot resist a pang of regret in thinking she might have been mistress of Pemberley. The park and house combine a natural beauty and artistic good taste that reflect the values and character of their owner, and significantly contrast with the ostentation at Rosings. The impression they make is confirmed by all the housekeeper says. Despite his dislike of Wickham, Darcy allows Wickham's miniature portrait to remain in its place in his father's room, out of a respect he keeps quiet about. Wickham proclaims an identical respect, but dishonours it. Throughout this chapter Elizabeth is very agitated. She feels she should not be at Pemberley at all and is horrified at what construction Darcy might put on her being there when he unexpectedly turns up. Deeply moved by all she hears about Darcy, she 'longs to hear more'; she 'longs to know' what he now thinks of her; she 'longs' to explore the estate. Clearly, her feelings towards him are quickening and deepening. To an extent, Darcy has changed, as Elizabeth repeatedly tells herself. What she doesn't realise is that her perception of him has changed very largely because *she* has changed. The Gardiners – her spiritual parents – have so far heard only good of Wickham and bad of Darcy, but behave with exemplary tact throughout, despite their astonishment.

Chapter 44

Summary
Earlier than expected, Darcy brings his sister to meet Elizabeth, convincing the Gardiners of his love for their niece. Bingley comes, too, and Elizabeth is quick to note that he shows no indication of being in love with Georgiana, but gives gratifying hints of still caring for Jane. Wickham is shown in a still worse light by local report. Elizabeth analyses her feelings for Darcy and acknowledges how grateful she feels for the constancy of his love, and questions herself as to whether she should encourage 'a renewal of his addresses'.

Commentary
Elizabeth has heard that Georgiana is 'exceedingly proud'. Perhaps the lessons she has recently learned enable her to see that Georgiana is, in fact, 'only exceedingly shy'. With the change she continues to see in Darcy, the vocabulary in which she thinks of him is altered. He is now, when she looks back, thought of as having been 'an acute and unembarrassed' observer; but at the time, she thought him 'proud', 'arrogant' and 'insolent'.

Chapter 45

Summary
Elizabeth and her aunt call on Georgiana the next day. The Bingley sisters are there, and Caroline runs true to form by her cold and critical treatment of Elizabeth. Darcy cannot resist joining their company, and this provokes Caroline, who is as jealous as ever, into sneering at Elizabeth's family. What she does not know is that her half-veiled reference to Wickham is more hurtful to Darcy and his sister than to Elizabeth. When she leaves, Elizabeth is viciously attacked by Caroline, who reminds Darcy of his uncomplimentary first impression of her. Provoked, Darcy openly declares his admiration for Elizabeth.

Commentary
Elizabeth comes well out of her encounter with Caroline Bingley. Because she is unaware of the secret they share about Wickham, Caroline's efforts to alienate Elizabeth from Darcy and his sister ironically misfire, and actually *unite* them. Her attempt to shame Darcy by recalling unfavourable remarks he initially made about Elizabeth has the desperation of someone who is conscious that she is losing the struggle to secure Darcy for herself. Her persistence forces Darcy into openly declaring what she

least wants to hear. Given Elizabeth's changed feelings about Darcy, everything now points to a renewed proposal and a happy conclusion.

Chapter 46

Summary

Next day brings disaster. Two letters arrive from Jane. The first tells of Lydia's elopement with Wickham. They are to marry at Gretna Green. The second letter dashes this hope by telling of Colonel Forster's visit to Longbourn. Lydia has brought disgrace on herself and her family. When Darcy calls on her, Elizabeth reveals everything to him. He is shocked, and after ensuring she is safely in the hands of the Gardiners, takes his leave. Elizabeth admits to herself that she could love Darcy, but does so at the very point when she believes that this last disgrace in her family must forever rule out the possibility of his marrying her. Together with the Gardiners she leaves hastily for home.

Commentary

In an age much more formal than our own, Lydia's behaviour was thought to be scandalous in the extreme and a disgrace to her entire family. This helps to explain why the hypochondriacal Mrs Bennet retreats to her bed, while her husband drops his witty posing and dashes off to London in 'excessive distress' in an ineffectual effort to track down the couple. We are reminded of Elizabeth's attempt to get her father to discipline Lydia in Chapter 41. Elizabeth herself is overcome with self-reproach for not having revealed more about what she knew about Wickham to her family. Darcy must appreciate that her reticence was out of loyalty to him. Her distress, intense as it is, is shared with Darcy, and is actually to strengthen their intimacy, though she cannot see this, and actually *mis*understands, when she thinks she understands, his 'gloomy' reaction. Significantly, the prospect of losing him brings the realisation that she could love Darcy.

Chapter 47

Summary

Elizabeth is not convinced by her uncle's arguments that Wickham must marry Lydia and reveals some of what she knows about his bad character; nor can she have faith in Lydia. They arrive at Longbourn to find Mrs Bennet melodramatically depressed after her earlier hysterics. Mr Bennet writes from London, but has nothing to report. Mary moralises ridiculously, and Kitty is unhelpful and fretful. Jane has clearly been the mainstay of the family, helped by her Aunt Philips. She produces the note left for Mrs Forster by Lydia. It is deplorably silly and immature.

Commentary

Elizabeth's realism is shown in several ways. She knows Wickham will 'never marry a woman without some money'; she recognises her father's weakness and what it has led to; she continues to blame herself (unlike her mother who blames everyone *except* herself); she guesses that the matter will have been indiscreetly discussed in front of the servants and, unlike Jane, who is too prone to believe the best of everyone, she knows that Lady Lucas's visit had less to do with offering genuine help than with rivalry and an impulse to triumph over the Bennets' misfortune. Mrs Bennet rails against the villainous Wickham, but pleads with her brother to '*make* them marry', none the less; and in her distress, her mind still runs on wedding clothes and 'the best warehouses'.

Chapter 48

Summary

Mr Gardiner leaves to assist Mr Bennet in his futile search. There are more reports on what a blackguard Wickham is. Collins writes a priggish and hypocritical letter of 'consolation' to the family, labouring how their disgrace must harm 'all the daughters'. After his fruitless search, Mr Bennet comes home. He admits his blame for what has happened.

Commentary

In Meryton, where his reputation was so high, Wickham is now spoken of as 'the wickedest young man in the world.' Collins's letter is that of a Job's comforter. A Christian clergyman, he writes in terms that parody the parable of the prodigal son: 'throw off your unworthy child from your affection forever'. Every word in the letter drives home the family disgrace, and he virtually congratulates himself for having escaped scandal by not marrying Elizabeth. Mr Bennet, even in the act of acknowledging his blame, is aware of his limited capacity to face up to it properly. His wit persists, though it is turned against himself in his recognition that he is not 'overpowered' by guilt, and that 'it will pass away soon enough' – as it does.

Chapter 49

Summary

A letter from Mr Gardiner declares that Lydia and Wickham have been traced. Moreover, Wickham has agreed to marry Lydia for a settlement that Elizabeth and her father think suspiciously small. They suppose Mr Gardiner must have offered additional money of his own. They also see through the pretence that a marriage arrived at in this way can be a source of satisfaction, let alone delight, as it is for Mrs Bennet.

Commentary

The responses of the characters to the news are very revealing. Mrs Bennet is beside herself with delight and can talk of nothing but the wonder of it, the wedding clothes and 'how merry' it all is. Jane congratulates her father and thinks Wickham 'not so undeserving', despite the mercenary deal he has made; indeed, her good sense tells her that her uncle could not afford to buy Wickham off with a large sum, so she naively believes that Wickham settles for less out of affection for Lydia. Elizabeth and her father clearly perceive the moral issue. Mr Bennet ironically does Wickham the credit of assuming he is a venal blackguard, not a fool. Elizabeth is sickened by the folly of her mother's dashing off to triumph over her rival Lady Lucas with the 'good news' that the couple are to marry, 'small as is their chance of happiness, and wretched as is his character'. If anything can justify Mr Bennet's total contempt for his wife, it is her response to the news.

Chapter 50

Summary

Mr Bennet fulfils his own prophecy of himself and reverts to indolence. He has been a poor manager of his money in the past and has come out of this crisis with little inconvenience to himself. Even his resolve not to permit Lydia and Wickham into his home will be abandoned. Meanwhile, Elizabeth comes to realise the full extent of her love for Darcy, hopeless though it now seems, since he could never stoop to marry into a family that includes Wickham. Wickham is to be posted to the North, to the relief of everyone except Mrs Bennet.

Commentary

Detailed consideration is given to the significant part money plays in a marriage. The Collinses' marriage has already been exposed as materially satisfactory but wholly loveless; Lydia's and Wickham's marriage is neither materially satisfactory nor based on any true respect for, or understanding of, one another's character. The Bennets' marriage, based originally in physical attraction, is one of disastrous incompatibility. Aware of all that can be wrong with marriage, Elizabeth acknowledges with regret that if (impossibly) she and Darcy were to marry, they would be complementary and ideally suited partners.

Chapter 51

Summary

Lydia and Wickham return to Longbourn married. They are unabashed: Lydia is tastelessly triumphant, even offering, as a married woman, to find her older sisters husbands, while Wickham is all artificial charm. Clearly, the Gardiners did not share Lydia's sense of elopement and marriage as being in any way 'fun'. In her thoughtless chattering, Lydia startles Elizabeth by letting out the secret that Darcy attended her wedding.

Commentary

Lydia has high spirits and low intelligence. Her self-assurance is at least spontaneous (everything is an exciting game to her); but Wickham's self-assurance is artificial and studied. Elizabeth is quick to see that Lydia's affection is not matched by his. She cannot bear their moral blindness to their position, leaves their company in protest, and twice voices her direct criticism, stating she does not like Lydia's 'way of getting husbands', and declaring 'there cannot be too little said' on the subject of their marriage. Darcy's having been at the wedding holds out a hope that Elizabeth seizes on eagerly.

Chapter 52

Summary

The letter from her aunt gives Elizabeth an account of Darcy's part in finding Lydia and Wickham, in vainly trying to persuade Lydia to return home, and finally in paying off Wickham's debts and bribing him into marriage. Mr Gardiner feels uneasy about the secrecy involved, especially since he is given praise for Darcy's generosity. Elizabeth feels humble, confronted by Darcy's sheer goodness. Her aunt clearly hints it has all been done for love of Elizabeth, but she dares not let herself believe this. In her encounter with Wickham, she lets him know that she has seen through all his misrepresentations, and succeeds in disconcerting him, if not in obtaining his admission of having lied. Out of good nature, she hopes they will see eye to eye in the future.

Commentary

Wickham is confirmed as a fortune hunter, not especially interested in Lydia. His approach to his 'dear sister' Elizabeth can be variously interpreted. Is he insensitively trying to get back on to his former footing with her, as if nothing had happened? Is he trying to find out how much she knows? Is he hoping for some sign of her forgiveness and future support?

Elizabeth both by direct reference to the housekeeper's comment and through some pointed hints makes her position clear, and we see from her handling of him how much she has matured. The kindness of her last remark can only be fully grasped when we recollect that Wickham is the real obstacle to her happiness, since she cannot believe Darcy could endure being brother-in-law to Wickham.

Chapter 53

Summary

Lydia and Wickham leave for Newcastle. Life seems to be settling into a routine monotony when news comes that Bingley will shortly return to Netherfield, and before long he and Darcy call at Longbourn to pay their respects. Bingley's interest in Jane is not dead, after all, and Darcy has clearly withdrawn his disapproval. Elizabeth is still unsure of Darcy's love for her. She undergoes agonies of embarrassment at the way her mother, unconscious of how much the family owes to Darcy, treats him with disrespect.

Commentary

Wickham's affectionate farewells lead Mr Bennet to wonder whether he or Sir William Lucas can 'produce a more valuable son-in-law'. It is hard to choose between a blackguard and an utter fool! A year has passed, but Mrs Bennet's efforts to get her husband to visit Netherfield, now that Bingley is returning, recapitulate the opening of the novel. This time, however, Mr Bennet means it when he refuses. The Bennet sisters are still uncertain of where they stand with their admirers, but Bingley and Darcy are similarly uncomfortable from not knowing where they stand with Jane and Elizabeth.

Chapter 54

Summary

Bingley and Darcy come to dinner at Longbourn. It is plain that Bingley is very much attracted to Jane. Elizabeth agitatedly hopes that Darcy, who seems gloomy and reticent, will sit next to her at dinner and seize the opportunity to talk to her, but she meets with repeated frustrations.

Commentary

The relationship between Bingley and Jane is renewed, free of all obstacles, and Elizabeth feels a 'triumphant sensation' at the happiness in store for them. By contrast, there are impediments still in her relationship with Darcy: not only the annoying seating arrangements, but also Darcy's apparent gloom, though this is really the outcome of shyness and uncertainty. Elizabeth's lack of composure and anger with herself for expecting a renewal of Darcy's love typfies the insecurity she feels so intensely just because she now knows how much she needs him.

Chapter 55

Summary

Once Darcy has left for London, Mrs Bennet schemes more actively than ever to throw Bingley and Jane together, and since Bingley is only too willing to co-operate, they become engaged. Their marriage, Elizabeth sees, will be happy because it has a foundation of affection, compatibility of mind and temperament, and of course material security. Mr Bennet approves, but shrewdly warns them that their easy dispositions could be exploited by others. Jane now understands that Caroline Bingley has acted against her and tells Elizabeth, who conceals from her Darcy's influence in keeping the lovers apart.

Commentary

Elizabeth is delighted that Jane and Bingley are in love, but even at this point, when she loves Darcy and knows how generous he can be, entertains a last suspicion that he could return and spoil their romance. When Jane is engaged, she cannot believe she deserves so much happiness, and very typically she wants everyone to be as happy as she is. Mrs Bennet, after her farcical scheming to ensure that Jane and Bingley are left on their own, is overjoyed by their engagement. Jane suddenly becomes her favourite, and Wickham and Lydia are forgotten. The engagement resolves the sub-plot.

Chapter 56

Summary

Having heard a rumour that Darcy intends to marry Elizabeth, Lady Catherine arrives unexpectedly at Longbourn, where she snubs Mrs Bennet and tries to persuade, browbeat and bully Elizabeth into giving her an assurance that she is not engaged to Darcy, and never will be. Elizabeth outwits Lady Catherine in her answers and finally tells her very frankly to mind her own business.

Commentary

We enjoy the wit with which Elizabeth puts down Lady Catherine, as when she wonders at Lady Catherine's taking the trouble to come so far to protest about a rumour she has pronounced to be untrue and unbelievable. Lady

Catherine's arguments are based on pride, privilege, birth and snobbery, not on reason or good sense. Elizabeth declares herself, as 'a gentleman's daughter', Darcy's equal. When Lady Catherine becomes threateningly abusive about Lydia, Elizabeth abandons wit and speaks with a concise frankness that shows how able she is to speak up for herself and control the situation she finds herself in. Lady Catherine goes off to report Elizabeth's 'insolence' to Darcy, and ironically her account gives him courage to propose a second time.

Chapter 57

Summary
Elizabeth's speculations on how Lady Catherine came to hear of a supposed engagement between Darcy and herself are confirmed when her father shows her a letter he has received from Collins. It carries congratulations on Jane's engagement to Bingley, then sternly warns against any relationship between Elizabeth and Darcy, since such a connection could be socially disgraceful and offensive to Lady Catherine. The letter goes on to condemn Lydia with excessive harshness, and concludes with the news of Charlotte's pregnancy. Mr Bennet disconcerts Elizabeth by assuming the rumour concerning herself and Darcy to be 'delightfully absurd'.

Commentary
The reader, like Elizabeth, suffers a sense of anti-climax when Mr Bennet reveals that Collins, not Darcy, has written the letter. Collins, who always has an eye on the main chance, assumes that Elizabeth will 'take immediate advantage' of Darcy's offer, and is aware that this will damage his own advancement, which depends on his pleasing Lady Catherine. Elizabeth's uncertainty about Darcy's intentions makes it painfully impossible for her to explain her position to her father, who treats what Collins has to say as an absurd joke.

Chapter 58

Summary
Darcy and Bingley return to Longbourn and in the course of a walk Elizabeth and Darcy find themselves on their own. Elizabeth decides to give Darcy an opening for declaring his feelings and begins by revealing her knowledge of, and gratitude for, what he has done to save Lydia from shame. Unaware that she knew this secret, Darcy is caught off guard. He admits that what he did was done for her sake alone, and confesses his

feelings for her have remained constant. She admits her own feelings for him have changed, at which encouragement he openly declares his love. They each confess the pride and prejudice they have had to overcome: in particular, he has been tortured by the reproof that he had failed to behave 'in a gentleman-like manner', and she has suffered the shame of having to admit that she so persistently and unfairly misjudged his character and actions. It is clear that Darcy has brought Bingley and Jane together again.

Commentary

This chapter is the climax of the novel and resolves the main plot. Ironically, Lady Catherine's efforts to separate Darcy from Elizabeth unite him with her. But Darcy behaves here in dramatic contrast to his behaviour when he first proposed: he is tentative, unsure of himself, in need of Elizabeth's encouragement. The pride he admits to, that dates back to his early upbringing, has been humbled. He confesses that Elizabeth has 'taught [him] a lesson'; but Elizabeth too has learned many lessons and has humbly come to a better understanding of herself. Jane Austen, with typical restraint, avoids dialogue at the very climax of the novel, giving the reader just enough detail for the imagination to work on. The fact that we are not given impassioned speech by no means indicates any lack of passion. It is worth noting that when Darcy expresses his love, Elizabeth is unable 'to encounter his eye', and they come back to Longbourn very late, having lost their direction and all sense of time in their absorption with each other.

Chapter 59

Summary

Elizabeth has difficulty in getting Jane to accept that her engagement to Darcy results from genuine love of him, and predictably the difficulty increases when, after Darcy has seen Mr Bennet, her father asks her to explain herself. He shows a sincere concern for her, and takes some convincing that Elizabeth knows what she is doing. Darcy's part in settling with Wickham is also explained. Mrs Bennet's view that Darcy is 'disagreeable' is immediately reversed once he is engaged to Elizabeth.

Commentary

Jane's reproach that Elizabeth has been 'very sly, very reserved' is true, since Elizabeth feared to speak of her changed feelings for Darcy until she was sure of his feelings for her. Everyone in the family has been taken in by her dislike of Darcy, which though once apparent, has for some time ceased to be real. The clue to Mr Bennet's concern for his favourite is his insistence that she should marry someone she can respect and so avoid (as he himself failed to avoid) an 'unequal marriage'. When he learns of Darcy's settling with Wickham, he reverts to a practical cynicism that does him little credit: as ever, he is delighted not to have to do anything. Mrs Bennet's changed view of Darcy is farcical and relates to a wholly false set of values. Marriage has no meaning for her beyond pin-money, jewels and carriages.

Chapter 60

Summary
Elizabeth and Darcy continue to analyse how their relationship developed, filling in gaps in their knowledge of each other. They write very different letters to their respective aunts, Elizabeth declaring herself 'the happiest creature in the world', Darcy announcing an engagement so unacceptable to Lady Catherine that the Collinses pay a visit to Lucas Lodge to escape her fury. Mr Bennet's letter to Collins satirically advises him to 'stand by the nephew', who has 'more to give'!

Commentary
When we left Elizabeth and Darcy at the end of Chapter 58, she was re-straining her impulse to tease Darcy. In this chapter, her playfulness reasserts itself, and she clearly intends to teach Darcy to laugh at himself. She teases him with the accusation that her attraction for him lay exclusively in her being unlike his flattering admirers, especially Caroline Bingley. Her embarassment over her mother's and Aunt Philips's social ineptness is added to when her cousin, Collins, visits the district again. She protects Darcy as much as possible from these relations for whom she feels such shame, even though he has learned greater tolerance; and she cannot wait to exchange her vulgar connections for 'the comfort and elegance' that waits her at Pemberley.

Chapter 61

Summary
Darcy and Elizabeth are fulfilled in each other at Pemberley. Their happi-ness is enhanced when Bingley and Jane buy a house nearby. Kitty is educated into better ways by her sisters, and Mary, free from competition from her prettier sisters, stops being so bookish. Lydia and Wickham are

spongers, living a restless and hollow marriage. Georgiana lives at Pemberley on the friendliest terms with her sister-in-law. Caroline Bingley, rather than be shut off from visiting Pemberley, cultivates both Jane and Elizabeth. Lady Catherine eventually condescends to forgive her nephew and satisfy her curiosity by visiting Pemberley. Mr Bennet is a frequent visitor, as are the well-liked Gardiners.

Commentary

The chapter supplies a conventional summary of what lies ahead for the main characters, all very much in keeping with our expectations.

3 THEMES

3.1 MARRIAGE

The dominant theme here, as in other of Jane Austen's novels, is marriage: her art is to focus critically on a few genteel characters who are affected by the progress of two or more of their number coming together in courtship, meeting with difficulties, eventually resolving them, and marrying happily at last. In *Pride and Prejudice* three marriages are made, other than that of Elizabeth and Darcy, and each in its way sheds light on the marriage of hero and heroine; but so, too, do some other long-standing marriages, especially that of Mr and Mrs Bennet.

There is a majestic ring about the novel's opening sentence:

> It is a truth universally acknowledged, that a single man in possession of a good fortune must be in want of a wife.

The marriage theme is clearly stated (or amusingly overstated), but we have only to read on a page or two to realise how little there is of majesty in the marriage of the cynically witty Mr Bennet and his vulgar wife, full of schemes to marry off her five daughters. Despite his perverse teasing, Mr Bennet shares his wife's concern to find husbands for their daughters, since the girls are without fortune or security, and marriage is the only hope for their future.

At the time when Jane Austen wrote, marriage was thought to be the single possible fulfilment for a woman. Careers were not open for middle- and upper-class women, who, except for the few with independent means, were forced to find husbands from sheer economic necessity. Those who succeeded had their status in society determined by the social and financial standing of their husbands. Those who failed sank into genteel poverty or suffered the humiliation of being 'placed' in families as governesses on the recommendation of Lady Catherine de Bourgh, or someone like her (see Chapter 29).

Unless we understand this, we cannot fully appreciate the supreme confidence of Mr Collins, ludicrous, pompous and unattractive as he is, in offering his hand to Elizabeth; nor the independence of spirit Elizabeth shows in her rejection of him, not to mention her rejection of Darcy and his £10,000 a year. Collins well knows that, in the world's eyes, Elizabeth is in no position to refuse him, and this, as much as his conceit and obtuseness, leads him not to take her refusal seriously. When he later proposes to Charlotte Lucas, who is as worldly and calculating as himself, and who accepts that marriage is 'the only honourable provision' for a young woman without means, she wastes no time in accepting him. But *all* Charlotte is looking for is security. She sees happiness in marriage as 'entirely a matter of chance', though she must know her chance of finding it with Collins is extremely slender. If she comes anywhere near it, she does so by *avoidance* of her husband, taking refuge at the rear of the parsonage, much as Mr Bennet escapes to his library from his despised wife.

While Charlotte's loveless marriage is a grim example to Elizabeth, so too is the apparently 'romantic' marriage of Lydia and Wickham. Though she shares the 'quick parts' of her father, there is sufficient of her mother in Elizabeth for her to respond, superficially at least, to the sham charm and scarlet uniform of Wickham. When she elopes, Lydia in a sense acts out and carries to an exaggerated conclusion Elizabeth's own romantic impulses. She is, of course, unthinking and irresponsible, and shielded by silliness from seeing Wickham for the blackguard he really is. But Elizabeth has taken his measure, realises that he does not care for Lydia, and that Lydia's love, which is no more than physical attraction, cannot long survive marriage to a spendthrift husband about whose character she is ignorant. Her own parents' marriage, also based on highly perishable 'youth and beauty', has miserably failed, though it got off to a much better start than Lydia's, both in terms of mutual attraction and material security.

From the examples before her, Elizabeth sees that neither marriage for security alone, nor marriage based on physical attraction alone, can hold out any possibility of success; nor has she the least respect for the old, aristocratic convention, represented by Lady Catherine de Bourgh, whereby marriages are to be arranged, not with regard to the individuals involved, but for the sake of promoting the material prosperity of their families. The union between Lady Catherine's daughter and Darcy may have been decided when they were 'in their cradles', but Elizabeth rejects a code of 'honour, decorum, prudence. . .interest' that is drawn up without reference to herself in such a way as to deprive her of any rights whatever. As Elizabeth tells Lady Catherine, 'the world in general' has too much sense to take notice of so antiquated a convention (see Chapter 56). This ought not to suggest, however, that Elizabeth, or Jane Austen, is indifferent to the important role marriage has to play in society, the sane ordering of which depends on couples who choose one another with wisdom, so that in achieving their own fulfilment they are also, as responsible parents, guaranteeing society's future stability. Significantly, the focus of the last chapter of the novel is not on the couples themselves so much as on their interrelationships and social roles.

Turning now to positive examples, we see in the Gardiner's marriage a happiness that is built on mutual understanding, trust and liking. Between Elizabeth's aunt and uncle is an *equality* that is wholly missing in her parents' marriage, as Mr Bennet well understands; indeed, he is never more serious and sincere than in warning Elizabeth against entering on an 'unequal marriage' (Chapter 59). Jane and Bingley, too, afford an example of marriage at its best. Their courtship suffers temporary setbacks, but these come about because of the interference of others, not because of any absence of trust or affection on their part. Their marriage has a rational foundation based in 'the excellent understanding, and super-excellent disposition of Jane, and a general similarity of feeling and taste' between them (Chapter 55). It has also a sound economic foundation. Such obstacles as exist to the happy union of Jane and Bingley are imposed from without. Once removed, their fulfilment in one another is guaranteed.

Unlike Jane and Bingley, Elizabeth and Darcy in their courtship are beset not with external obstacles that are imposed, but with obstacles rooted within their own natures. In terms of a distinction Elizabeth makes (Chapter 9), her sister and Bingley are uncomplicated in character, whereas Darcy, like herself, has 'a deep intricate character', and both of them have to be subjected to a long, thorough process of learning about themselves and one another before they can enter on a marriage of true minds and true hearts in the expectation of 'rational happiness'. There is an obvious inequality between them, but this is confined to wealth alone. As Elizabeth proudly asserts, in argument with Lady Catherine, Darcy 'is a gentleman; I am a gentleman's daughter: so far we are equal' (Chapter 56). But they are well matched intellectually, too, as their repartee indicates, and share independence of spirit and judgement. Their intricate characters, inclining both of them to pride and prejudice, plunge them into misunderstanding, and only at the end of the novel, after a chastening experience of one another, are they sure of their deep affection and moral and temperamental compatibility. He no longer proposes to Elizabeth as to an inferior, insensitively ignoring her as someone with an identity of her own and a proper pride of her own, but offers himself very tentatively and even humbly. She for her part has rid herself of the prejudice and largely imaginary wrongs that blinded her to Darcy's merits, and is no less humble in the gratitude and love she has for him. But while their marriage is built on respect, understanding, compatibility and a secure economic basis, it by no means lacks affection and even passion. Darcy's 'bewitchment' is real enough, and even if he insults Elizabeth with his first proposal, we cannot doubt the strength of feeling that drives him into making it. Meanwhile, it can be argued that Elizabeth's determined efforts to hate Darcy point to a deep emotional involvement that frightens her; that the depth and strength of this involvement is more significant than the fact that it is negative; and that all such feeling is ambiguous, so that the shift in her feeling from passionate hate to love is psychologically convincing.

3.2 PARENTAL RESPONSIBILITY

A further theme in the novel is that of parental responsibility, though it is explored in negative, rather than positive, terms. The only positive example showing this kind of responsibility being wisely exercised comes not from Elizabeth's parents, but from her aunt and uncle, whose sympathy, tact and practical good sense entitle them to be considered her spiritual parents. As for Mr and Mrs Bennet, they offer between them a convincing and comprehensive example of parental irresponsibility. Mr Bennet has made the grave mistake of marrying a woman who had nothing whatever to commend her except a pretty face. Instead of accepting his mistake and making the best of it by giving their children the support they very much need in view of their mother's ignorance, stupidity, hypochondria and vacuous values, he has withdrawn himself physically and psychologically from wife and family alike. Basically, he is lazy and always takes the easy way out of his difficulties, or refuses even to face them. His sharp wit itself is used as a defence against any demand made on him, however just that demand may be.

The clearest exposition of the failure of both Mr and Mrs Bennet as parents is given in Chapter 41. Lydia is invited to Brighton, and her mother is uncritically delighted, and indeed, envious. Knowing how futile it would be to talk to her mother, who has no more sense than to give her rapturous approval, Elizabeth seeks out her father and represents to him 'all the improprieties of Lydia's general behaviour' and the imprudence, in particular, of allowing her to be exposed, with so little protection, to all the temptations of Brighton. Her father typically falls back on his wit to justify taking the easiest course:

> Lydia will never be easy till she has exposed herself in some public place or other, and we can never expect her to do it with so little expense or inconvenience to her family as under the present circumstances.

Again Elizabeth presses him to consider 'the very great disadvantage' that the whole family must suffer as a consequence of Lydia's giddy behaviour. Though she does not openly state that Jane's chances with Bingley have been ruined because of her younger sisters' imprudence, she warns her father that how they behave reflects badly on herself and Jane. The irony here lies in the reversal of roles: the twenty-year-old girl is having to speak like a parent to her father, while he childishly abandons all reponsibility and treats her warnings as an occasion for self-indulgent amusement:

> . . .What, has she frightened away some of your lovers? Poor little Lizzy! But do not be cast down. Such squeamish youths as cannot bear to be connected with a little absurdity are not worth a regret.

Mr Bennet concedes that Elizabeth has 'three very silly sisters', but without accepting the least responsibility for them; and having insisted that there will be 'no peace' if Lydia is not given her head, he closes discussion with a typical quip, declaring Lydia 'cannot grow many degrees worse, without authorising us to lock her up for the rest of her life'. When Elizabeth's warnings prove all too true and Lydia elopes, Mr Bennet is, for once, shaken into uncustomary action, though his efforts are, as we might expect, wholly futile. Returning to Longbourn, he confides in Elizabeth that he *deserves* to suffer for his irresponsibility, but even here, in the act of acknowledging he is at fault, he is aware of his strictly limited capacity to face up to his own guilt:

> . . .I am not afraid of being overpowered by the impression. It will pass away soon enough.' (Chapter 48).

And indeed, it does. He is hardly better than his superficial and mindless wife in accepting that others should make a settlement and resolve the scandal of the elopement for him; and far from feeling shame that others should pay for his mistakes, when everything is finally revealed all he can do is exclaim: 'So much the better. It will save me a world of trouble and economy.' (Chapter 59). Even his resolve not to admit Lydia and Wickham to his home is not kept, and we are left in no doubt as to his being a self-indulgent, quirky and ineffectual parent. Apart from his panic response to the elopement, the only other occasion when he shows a father's concern is when Elizabeth tells him of her intention to marry Darcy. Speaking sincerely for once, out of the misery of his own experience, he then begs her not to repeat his own mistake by making 'an unequal marriage' (Chapter 59). There is no evidence to show that either he or his wife is aware that their children are in any way victims of a disastrous marriage (though to be fair, Mrs Bennet is too stupid to see her marriage *is* disastrous).

3.3 SOCIETY

Another recurrent theme relates to society and its conventions. Society itself is satirised on several occasions. Bingley's praises are loudly sung, but diminish when at the Meryton ball Darcy appears and puts him in the shade with 'his fine, tall person, handsome features, noblemen' and, of course, his ten thousand pounds a year. But once Darcy is seen 'to be proud, to be above his company', public opinion immediately turns its praises into condemnation and reinstates Bingley as a favourite (Chapter 3). A similar, if more drawn out, instance of society's superficial and fickle judgement occurs when the universally popular Wickham leaves debts behind him. Not only does everyone in Meryton declare him to be 'the wickedest young man in the world', but they belatedly recollect 'that they had always distrusted the appearance of his goodness' (Chapter 48). Jane Austen's bitterest satire on society comes in Chapter 50, where the vicious gossip against Lydia is disappointingly curtailed by her marriage, although:

> . . .the good-natured wishes for her well-doing, which had proceeded before from all the spiteful old ladies of Meryton, lost but little of their spirit in this change of circumstances, because with such a husband, her misery was considered certain.

Elizabeth in particular is willing to disregard the sillier social conventions. No properly brought up young lady was expected to walk 'above her ankles in dirt', but the Bingley sisters' condemnation of Elizabeth's mud-died petticoat is exposed as reprehensible snobbishness by Bingley himself, who sees that sisterly affection matters far more than 'decorum'. Time after time, Elizabeth challenges by her wit and good sense the pretentions of Lady Catherine, and refuses to be impressed by claims that are based in social status rather than in the merits of the individual. Lydia's patched-up marriage may satisfy convention and authorise Lydia's claim to a superior position to her older sisters at the dining table, but Elizabeth and her father are sickened by the hypocrisy of it.

3.4 APPEARANCE AND REALITY

The themes of courtship and marriage, of parenthood and of social convention are all comprehended in the broadest theme of all: that of appearance and reality, which itself is integrated in the total moral perspective of the novel. People are often far from being what they appear to be. Outwardly, Collins is a Christian clergyman, but he is by nature a sycophant and social climber, implacably without charity; Mr Hurst is outwardly a gentleman, but is basically a glutton and a philistine; the fashionable and ladylike Bingley sisters can hardly wait for their door to close on Elizabeth before coarsely criticising her for having the same connections with trade as they themselves have, but hypocritically ignore; and as for Darcy and Wickham, 'one has got all the goodness, and the other all the appearance of it' (Chapter 40). But a failure in self-knowledge, if not actual self-deception, also belongs to the appearance and reality theme. Both Darcy and Elizabeth have to discover their own genuine selves, and this discovery keeps pace with their discovery of one another, as they learn to rid themselves of the illusions and misunderstandings created by their pride and prejudice. It is no exaggeration to say that appearance and reality determine the whole structure of the novel.

4 TECHNIQUES

4.1 PLOT AND STRUCTURE

The first two chapters give the marriage theme a good airing. It is in the third chapter, when they attend the ball at Meryton, that Elizabeth and Darcy, hero and heroine, meet; but at their first encounter, Darcy seems cast more as anti-hero or villain than hero. He personifies the pride of the title when in reply to Bingley's suggestion that he should dance with Elizabeth, he replies with inexcusable arrogance:

> . . .She is tolerable; but not handsome enough to tempt *me*; and I am in no humour at present to give consequence to young ladies who are slighted by other men.

Still less excusably, he says this loudly enough to ensure that Elizabeth hears it, and although she laughs it off, the insult rankles with her and is the source of the persistent prejudice she bears towards him. This contrived eavesdropping on which the whole plot depends is clumsy and strains our credulity more than anything else in a novel that is otherwise virtually perfect in its construction and truth to nature, and therefore refreshingly different from the far-fetched, unrealistic fiction of the period.

From this point on, Darcy, after each encounter with Elizabeth, is brought to the disconcerting realisation that he is increasingly in love with her. She, meanwhile, grows more and more hostile towards him, so that for the first half of the novel, right up to Darcy's proposal, both of them are repeatedly at cross-purposes, misunderstanding and misinterpreting one another. We, as readers, are amused by encounters in which both find evidence for their quite different positions by twisting the same objective actions and words to confirm their fixed beliefs. Elizabeth's prejudice, which comes from her hurt pride, disqualifies her judgement, which is generally penetrating. She can see at once through the Bingley sisters and Lady Catherine de Bourgh; but when she meets Wickham, who is the nearest thing the novel has to a villain, her resentment against Darcy is reinforced by his. In consequence, she stubbornly persists in making the hero into a villain and, by the same perverse logic, the villain into a hero. She is constantly tripping up on her own cleverness, turning Darcy's admiring looks into criticism, his compliments into slights, and his silences into proofs of his guilt over Wickham. Darcy, meanwhile, convinces himself that because he feels increasingly attracted to Elizabeth she must feel attracted to him.

When in Chapter 34 Darcy confidently proposes, appearance and reality are at the furthest remove from one another. Everything has built up to a climax that abruptly and dramatically exposes the gulf of misunderstanding between hero and heroine. From this point on, beginning with Darcy's letter, reality displaces false appearances, misunderstanding gives way to true understanding, and the whole movement of the first half of the novel is reversed as hero and heroine draw progressively closer to one another. Elizabeth comes to feel 'absolutely ashamed of herself', and in her admission that 'had [she] been in love' she 'could not have been more wretchedly blind', she begins to understand what the strength of her emotional involvement with Darcy really implies. For his part, Darcy is humbled by rejection and the accusation of his having behaved in an 'ungentlemanly' manner. When they again meet, it is clear where their new-found respect for each other will lead; but then comes the news of Lydia's elopement with Wickham, the disgrace of which Elizabeth thinks must make marriage with Darcy impossible. But what she fears must separate them becomes a bond between them: not only because Darcy's own sister nearly eloped with Wickham, but because Darcy can give Elizabeth a final, clinching proof of his love by tracking down Wickham and Lydia and arranging a marriage settlement. A further attempt to put an obstacle between hero and heroine is made by Lady Catherine, whose resolve to separate them ironically misfires and brings Darcy to Longbourn to repeat his proposal. This time, Elizabeth joyfully accepts him. The cleverly sustained suspense we have felt as to whether Elizabeth and Darcy can triumph over all difficulties and marry each other is at last resolved. The gap between appearance and reality has closed to a point where the two become one.

The sub-plot involving Jane and Bingley in some ways corresponds to the main plot, but there are significant differences. Jane's relationship with Bingley begins, as Elizabeth's does with Darcy, at the Meryton ball; but their attraction to one another is immediate, and it is other people, not themselves, who constitute an obstacle to their developing attachment. The theme of appearance and reality is given a new twist when Bingley is talked into mistaking Jane's touching modesty for indifference, though in fact it conceals her genuine love for him. Once the misunderstanding between them is cleared, there are no further obstacles to their happiness. Neither of them is an 'intricate' character, and they therefore serve as foils to the hero and heroine. The main and sub-plots overlap when Darcy persuades Bingley to leave Jane (an act that violently antagonises Elizabeth), and when he later persuades him to return to her (an act that deepens Elizabeth's love for him).

4.2 CHARACTERS AND CHARACTERISATION

Pride and Prejudice is brought vividly to life by a gallery of different and contrasting characters, most of whom are readily identifiable from their speech alone. Often, we have only to hear a few words to identify speaker and subject: 'she is all affability and condescension'; 'I could easily forgive *his* pride, if he had not mortified *mine*'; 'what pin-money, what jewels, what carriages you will have!'; 'my character has ever been celebrated for its sincerity and frankness'; 'I defy even Sir William Lucas himself, to produce a more valuable son-in-law'. If we cannot readily identify such distinctive snippets, we cannot have read the novel very attentively. It is in and through dialogue that we learn most about the characters: their style reveals them as, for example, vulgar (Mrs Bennet), pompous (Collins), uneducated (Lydia), sensitive (Jane), clever (Elizabeth and Mr Bennet). and Mr Bennet).

Of course, not all characters are, or need to be, equally realised. Jane and Bingley are simpler, less intricate characters than Darcy and Elizabeth, and for that reason are also less interesting; they are not realised in great depth because psychologically they have no great depth. They suffer setbacks at the hands of other, more intricate characters, while the intricate characters create their own problems, to the confusion of themselves and one another. Even then, it is fair to say that neither Darcy nor Wickham is anything like as fully realised as Elizabeth, through whom so much of the story is presented.

There are several minor characters, varying in intricacy and interest, but all essentially presented within a naturalistic tradition. Their range is impressive: Mr Bennet, the Gardiners, Charlotte Lucas, Colonel Fitzwilliam, the Bingley sisters and Lydia and Kitty Bennet. The variety of these characters and the contrasts they present add interest and richness to the novel. They are on the whole realistically conceived and credible, unlike the remaining characters – Mrs Bennet, Collins, Lady Catherine de Bourgh and Sir William Lucas – who are better regarded as caricatures, and who are less *individually* realised than portrayed exaggeratedly, as representative types. Much of the comedy in *Pride and Prejudice* is located in them, and in their interaction with each other, as well as with more naturalistic characters.

Very obviously, the plot of *Pride and Prejudice* lies more in the psychology of the characters than in external events. This is particularly true in respect of Elizabeth and Darcy. Even so, the novel's structure is affected by the characters from time to time. The fact that Mrs Gardiner comes from Derbyshire has some bearing on the story, and above all the shift of scene to Rosings, permitting further developments in the relationship between hero and heroine, depends on Collins's having Darcy's aunt for patron and Elizabeth's close friend, Charlotte, for his wife.

Elizabeth Bennet Less beautiful than her sister Jane, whom she loves without jealousy, Elizabeth is much more spirited and independent than a twenty-year-old young lady of her period would ordinarily be. She has the self-respect of a 'gentleman's daughter' and is impatient with pretention and merely stuffy conventions. At the same time, she understands the value of propriety and good taste as Lydia, who disregards all decent standards of conduct out of empty-headed vulgarity, does not. Elizabeth is her father's favourite and inherits his 'quick parts', on which she prides herself a little too much.

Her 'lively, playful disposition, which delighted in anything ridiculous' makes her attractive, well liked by women (her aunt and Charlotte Lucas in particular) and much admired by men. Her discernment is not always as acute as she imagines it (she misjudges Charlotte Lucas), and once her pride is hurt, as it is by Darcy's cutting remarks at the Meryton ball, it is badly clouded by prejudice in which she stubbornly persists, in the belief that she is being 'uncommonly clever'. Disregarding all evidence to the contrary, she is determined to believe the worst of Darcy and is completely taken in by appearances – most notably, by the handsome and plausible Wickham. Why her sense of justice and generally reliable judgement should abandon her – why she should so unreasonably twist every word and action of Darcy against him – may be less of a mystery if we reflect that from the time of the original insult at the Meryton ball, she harbours a profound, and profoundly ambiguous, resentment towards him. The significant and betraying thing about her more superficially 'romantic' attachment to Wickham and Colonel Fitzwilliam is the way in which she is most serious and intimate with them when she is prompting them to talk about Darcy. From the time she receives Darcy's letter, her eyes are opened, and she acknowledges that she never knew herself; but her intellectual acknowledgement of her own pride and prejudice comes much earlier than her understanding of her emotions, which shift gradually from hatred of Darcy to love of him, encouraged by his treating her as his equal, which she knows herself to be.

Despite her youth, she refuses to defer to Lady Catherine's rank, since it is unsupported by individual merit. Far from being brow-beaten by her into renouncing any claim to Darcy, she has enough sharp wit to out-argue her, and the moral courage to defy her. Certainly Elizabeth has faults, but they are, properly understood, faults of impulsive generosity, not meanness of spirit. With typical fair-mindedness, she admits her errors and struggles towards a mature self-knowledge that she acquires only towards the end of the novel.

Fitzwilliam Darcy Seen from the outside, Darcy tends to be stuffy and solemn, in keeping with his great pride. He contrasts sharply with Elizabeth by lacking all lightness of touch; he dislikes small talk and is 'too little yielding' in his attitude to others. Though given 'good principles', he admits to a spoiled childhood in which he was 'left to follow them in pride and conceit'. An aristocrat with ten thousand pounds a year, he quickly attracts criticism at the Meryton ball because of the aloof contempt he shows to the company at large, and he deservedly earns Elizabeth's resentment by deliberately insulting her.

Not wholly convincingly, we are told later that his rudeness and haughtiness are defensive: that contrary to appearances, he is basically shy, too serious by nature for the frivolities of society, too sincere in his feelings to be able to make the charming display of them that comes naturally to a hypocrite like Wickham. Initially we see Darcy as Elizabeth sees him (and she is very biased), but we are subsequently given more and more evidence of his true nature, culminating in the testimony of Mrs Reynolds, the housekeeper at Pemberley, who speaks of him as an ideal master and landlord, an excellent brother, a model of good nature and generosity. Meanwhile, the natural good taste of Pemberley itself is a powerful witness to the kind of man Darcy really is. In the end, Elizabeth has to acknowledge not only that he has been fairer to Wickham than Wickham deserves, but also that his part in bringing about a separation between Bingley and Jane was not malicious, but done out of a concern for his friend in the excusable belief that Jane was not in love.

Darcy resolves the disgrace of Lydia's elopement by a practical marriage-settlement, and does so secretly, though once the secret is exposed, it confirms the deep sincerity and constancy of his love for Elizabeth. He has come a long way in self-knowledge since he offended Elizabeth by his patronising proposal. His pride, but not his self-respect, has been humbled. He, like Elizabeth, has come to realise they *are* equals, as people; that his family, like hers, is not exempt from vulgarity (Lady Catherine and Mrs Bennet are sisters under the skin), and that there is a lot of truth in Elizabeth's bantering claim that she has 'always seen a great similarity in the turn of [their] minds' (Chapter 18). Both of them see through silly formalities and conventions; both take a pride in their discernment; both abhor vulgarity and, most importantly of all, both of them come to see through appearances and to share the same moral perspective.

There is some truth in Elizabeth's claim that her attraction for Darcy resulted from his being 'sick of civility, of deference, of officious attention' from women like Caroline Bingley (Chapter 60); he comes most alive in dialogue when challenged by Elizabeth's wit, but is rather rigid and wooden as a character. Like Elizabeth, we have hopes that, in return for the 'judgement, information and knowledge of the world' he brings in marriage, she will succeed in her effort to get him to relax and laugh more at himself.

Jane Bennet Jane is so beautiful, physically and by nature, that she is beyond the criticism of even Darcy and Caroline Bingley. Her 'sweetness and disinterestedness' may be 'really angelic' (Chapter 24), but this often makes her naïve in her judgements. She is too good-natured in herself to discover harm or bad nature in others, and this occasionally draws Elizabeth's mockery; 'the meaning of principle and integrity' cannot be leniently redefined to conform with Jane's tender-heartedness; but on occasion Jane's judgement can be sounder than Elizabeth's: 'Can his most intimate friends be so excessively deceived in him? Oh! no,' she says, protesting against Elizabeth's eagerness to believe the worst of Darcy (Chapter 17).

She has genuine modesty and humility and this prevents her from giving enough positive encouragement to Bingley, as the shrewd Charlotte Lucas is quick to see; indeed, her character lacks forcefulness of any kind, and her sufferings and delights are passive, never the result of action on her part. The same is true of Bingley, and Mr Bennet's congratulations on their engagement show perception as well as wit: 'You are each of you so com-plying, that nothing will ever be resolved on; so easy that every servant will cheat you' (Chapter 55). Typically, Jane at this point cannot be so happy without thinking of others and exclaiming 'Oh! Why is not everybody as happy?'

In sharp contrast with Elizabeth, Jane has the simplest of natures. She is far less conscious of the vulgarity and shortcomings of her family than Elizabeth, who agonises over them, and she is painfully slow in forcing herself to recognise what Elizabeth sees at a glance: that Caroline Bingley is two-faced and no real friend. Her courtship and marriage belong to the tradition of the sentimental novel. Hers is a love at first sight, as is Bingley's. External difficulties prevent it from running its smooth course, but in itself it is an unclouded romantic love. It has something child-like about it; but Jane herself is in many ways child-like. Perhaps this is why she is such a favourite with the Gardiners' children.

Charles Bingley He could hardly be better matched than to Jane, since he shares her good nature, is 'unaffectedly modest', and he is passive and acted upon, without ever acting himself. When Elizabeth makes a distinc-tion between characters who can be perfectly understood because of their simplicity and straightforwardness (not to say shallowness) and those who are deep and intricate, she is mentally contrasting him with Darcy, and he has just enough individuality to suspect that 'to be so easily seen through' may not be entirely a compliment (Chapter 9). He stands in contrast to Darcy in much the same way as Jane does to Elizabeth, and therefore is extrovert, unsnobbish, easily pleased by any company, uncritical of vul-garity and without any taste for books, learning or even long words. Very much as Elizabeth watches protectively over Jane, so Darcy protects Bingley and orders his life for him. Elizabeth's final reflection on Bingley is affectionately sarcastic, but justified. Critical of Darcy, even though she is in love with him, she 'longed to observe that Mr Bingley had been a most delightful friend; so easily guided that his worth was invaluable. . .' (Chap-ter 58).

Mr Bennet Superficially attractive and amusing, Mr Bennet is an intricate character and not what he seems. His marriage, based on sexual attraction, has proved disastrous and he takes no care to conceal from his children or anyone else the contempt he feels for his vulgarly stupid wife. Disillusioned by marrying in every sense beneath him, he diverts himself with books and with making fun of everyone about him. 'For what do we live, but to make sport for our neighbours, and laugh at them in return?' he asks; but the wit of this turns sour, since it is finally a statement that exposes the sterility, and even despair, he feels about life.

Far from giving his children the support they badly need, considering their impossible mother, he withdraws himself physically and psychologically from all parental responsibility. In Chapter 41, we see Elizabeth and her father in reverse roles: she pleads with him to curb Lydia and refuse her permission to go to Brighton, while he takes, as always, the childishly easy way out, jesting about Elizabeth's seriousness, and concluding discussion with a quip. He is, however, profoundly disturbed by Lydia's elopement, which shakes him into action, though his search proves futile, and in the end he is lazily and irresponsibly content to allow others to resolve his problems for him, and literally pay for his mistakes. He is self-indulgent and weak in character, quirky, ineffectual and so irresolute that he cannot carry through his vow not to permit Lydia and Wickham into his home.

The elopement sobers Mr Bennet, but he knows his own limitations in saying that his sense of guilt is not likely to overpower him for long. His serious self is revealed in the moral stance (identical to Elizabeth's) he takes to the patched-up wedding, and in his fatherly concern that his favourite daughter should avoid 'an unequal marriage' that would condemn her to the misery of a marriage like his own.

Mrs Bennet Mrs Bennet is more of a caricature than a rounded character. Her obsession is with marrying off her daughters, and all her attitudes and freely-given opinions relate to this. Collins is detestable to her because he will inherit Longbourn; but once he declares an interest in marrying one of her daughters, she warms to him and flatters him, only to revert to detestation when he marries Charlotte Lucas. Her attitude to Bingley, and more particularly Darcy, varies similarly. When Lydia, her favourite, who very much resembles her, elopes, Mrs Bennet collapses in hysterics, but recovers immediately at the news of the arranged marriage, treating it as a triumph, boasting of it to the neighbours, though to anyone of good sense it is obviously doomed to failure; and even Lydia ceases to count much with her, once the prospect of Jane's marriage arises.

Mrs Bennet is comic in conception, with her 'mean understanding, little information, and uncertain temper' (Chapter 1). She is too stupid to realise that her husband baits her contemptuously, that successful marriage is more than pin money, jewels and carriages, and that her rudeness and opinionated vulgarity torture Elizabeth with embarassment. Lacking any moral awareness, she is childish, self-centred, hypochondriacal and uncharitable in her judgement of everybody outside her family. Her efforts to match-make are melodramatic and grotesque. As a mother, she is a model of all that is to be avoided. Mrs Gardiner affords a sharp contrast with her, as Mr Gardiner does with Mr Bennet.

Lydia Bennet If Elizabeth is in many ways her father's daughter, Lydia is even more the daughter of her mother. Indeed Mrs Bennet, once pretty herself, and still fond of a soldier's uniform, relives her youth through Lydia, whom she encourages when what Lydia badly needs is discipline. Though only fifteen and the youngest daughter, Lydia has enough brazen self-assurance to insult Collins, chivvy Bingley about giving a ball and set the pace for Kitty, her older sister, in chasing after officers in the militia. She is ill-educated, ignorant, pushing, vulgarly amiable, physically well developed and sexually precocious. Convention and propriety mean nothing to her, and she is at the teenage stage where everything seems hilarious. 'I can hardly write for laughing,' she writes, when eloping with Wickham and bringing her whole family into disgrace (Chapter 47). At no point does she show the least moral awareness, let alone self-blame for her actions, and her brash behaviour when she comes as a bride to Longbourn is a testimony to her unremitting silliness and bad taste. Her romantic attachment to Wickham will not last long, but she does, in her vain and empty-head way, love him for his uniform and good looks.

Kitty Bennet Kitty could be Lydia's twin, slightly toned down; but she is more amenable than her sister and is caught sufficiently early to be educated into better ways by her older sisters after they marry.

Mary Bennet Mary is the least good-looking of the family and tries to make up for this by displaying intellectual and artistic accomplishments in which, sadly, she by no means excels. She has to be dissuaded from demonstrating her genius as a pianist and her attempts to speak with the moral gravity of Dr Johnson are grotesque enough to amuse her father, though kinder natures might incline to pity her.

William Collins In Collins we are given a caricature of a worldly clergy-man. A flatterer at Rosings, he brings a breathtaking conceit and pompous-ness to Longbourn, together with the offer of his hand. When Mrs Bennet deflects his attention from Jane, in whom Bingley is showing an interest, Collins switches his ardour to Elizabeth in the time it takes to stir the fire; and when Elizabeth offends his pride by rejecting him, he proposes within a day or two to Charlotte Lucas. The fact is, Lady Catherine de Bourgh, on whom he pins his hopes for advancement, has condescended to tell him he must marry, and he cannot be too quick in pleasing her by doing so. His proposal to Elizabeth, which seems worded to humiliate her, is the most famous and fatuous in literature. As he sees it, he is so highly desirable a 'catch', he cannot believe Elizabeth sincere in rejecting him. Being himself totally self-seeking, with his eye forever on the main chance, it is incomprehensible to him that his young cousin should turn down so materially advantageous an offer, especially when, as he so gallantly suggests, she may never get another! The manner of his proposal, in which he incongruously spells out his reasons for marriage before permitting himself to be 'run away' with by a lover's feelings, is rich in comedy and satire. His style, in conversation and in his letters, exposes him as a pretentious, hypocritical fool, who delights us by combining an extravagant sycophancy towards Lady Catherine with supreme self-importance. Though a Christian clergyman, Collins has neither charity nor compassion. When Lydia elopes, he writes a condescending letter of apparent consolation to Mr Bennet in terms that parody the parable of the prodigal son: 'throw off your unworthy child from your affection for ever'. In his sly reply, Mr Bennet advises him to 'stand by' Darcy, rather than Lady Catherine, because Darcy 'has more to give' (Chapter 60). We can be sure the advice was acted upon.

Lady Catherine de Brough No more fitting patron for Collins could possibly exist. An aristocrat, she upholds arranged marriages, superior breeding and unlimited snobbery. Elizabeth stands up to her because she cannot detect in her any *individual* virtue or talent, while Lady Catherine, convinced that social rank automatically confers individual distinction, fatuously claims that if only she had learned the piano she would have been 'a great proficient'! She is a caricature of all that is worst in rank and privilege. Her home, Rosings, is ostentatiously grand, as is her manner towards her social inferiors, into whose lives she believes she has a moral duty to intrude. As Elizabeth notes, 'nothing was beneath this Lady's attention, which could furnish her with an occasion of dictating to others' and the author's mockery of her reaches a comic pitch when the company gather round to hear her 'determine what weather they were to have tomorrow' (Chapter 29). Her proud assertion of good breeding exposes her total want of it, and Darcy comes to recognise that his aunt and Mrs Bennet are sisters under the skin. Ironically, her bullying efforts to separate Darcy and Elizabeth misfire and actually unite them.

Charlotte Lucas Charlotte is an 'intricate' character, not a caricature. Though she is seven years older than Elizabeth, it is no surprise that they are good friends: they both have a lively intelligence and wit which they enjoy bringing critically to bear on their society. What Elizabeth fails to understand is that behind Charlotte's witty asertion that 'it is better to know as little as possible of the defects' of a future husband, there is a grim seriousness. It is often said on Charlotte's behalf that a plain spinster of her age, likely to be left 'on the shelf', and fearful of declining into genteel poverty or worse, had no real option but to marry, no matter who proposed to her; and she herself sees marriage as 'the only honourable provision' for someone in her circumstances (Chapter 22). It is therefore argued that Elizabeth should not be shocked when Charlotte manipulates Collins into marrying her; but the fact is, Jane Austen herself satirises Charlotte for accepting a ridiculous fool 'from the pure and disinterested desire of an establishment' (Chapter 22). After all has been said, Charlotte *knowingly* degrades herself by marrying a caricature, not a man. She protests her unromantic realism, but surely Elizabeth's sense of outrage is justified when someone as clever, as acutely perceptive, and as capable of moral discrimination as Charlotte is, chooses a future in which she knows she will have to suppress all these qualities that constitute her identity and hypocritically pretend affection and respect for a husband she despises. She invites our pity, but as Elizabeth reflects when they part, she has acted 'with her eyes open' and while enough of the old Charlotte survives for her still to blush for her husband, she stoically refuses 'to ask for compassion' (Chapter 38).

George Wickham Wickham has an 'appearance greatly in his favour' and he uses his handsome looks, good physique and conversational charm to manipulate everyone he comes in contact with – shopkeepers, his fellow officers, the ladies in general and Elizabeth in particular. The truth is, he is deceitful, dissipated, a liar, a seducer twice over, and the fact that when other things fail he aspires to be a clergyman reinforces our awareness not only of his hypocrisy, but of the hypocrisy prevalent in the Church at this period. At first, his superficial attractions rouse a romantic response in Elizabeth, and he effortlessly takes her in by half truths, misrepresentations and claims on her pity and sense of justice. He is an embodiment of favourable but misleading impressions. In this, he contrasts with Darcy, who has 'all the goodness', while Wickham has 'all the appearance of it' (Chapter 40). Even after Elizabeth recognises that Wickham selfishly exploits others, she insists that he 'must always be her model of the amiable and pleasing', and her good opinion of him persists until she has undeniable proof of his being a liar and seducer – in fact, a melodramatic villain of the kind found in the romances of the period. Like Charlotte Lucas, he is morally aware, but he acts not only amorally, but ruthlessly. Even Lydia hardly merits a seduction so loveless and coldly calculating. After the elopement we may, like Elizabeth, blush at the way Lydia so insensitively flaunts her husband, but the shameless amiability he continues to display is more likely to make us turn pale.

Caroline Bingley Miss Caroline Bingley and her sister, Mrs Hurst, have pretentions to aristocratic refinement and good taste. They conceal the fact that their family fortune has come from trade, any connection with which they hypocritically disdain in others. Caroline Bingley has physical attraction, a proper education and all the social accomplishments considered suitable in a young lady of her class, and she is determined to rise still higher in society by bringing all her charms and arts to bear on Darcy, whom she desperately wishes to marry. She is 'proud and conceited' and the most transparent sort of snob. Long before Elizabeth admits to feeling anything but resentment towards Darcy, Caroline perceives her as a rival, and seizes every chance to demonstrate in front of Darcy her imagined superiority over Elizabeth. Meanwhile, she vulgarly criticises Elizabeth behind her back, tiresomely jokes with Darcy about the prospect of a mother-in-law like Mrs Bennet, shamelessly praises him to his face and pretends to share his tastes. Ironically, Darcy is attracted by Elizabeth's refusal to flatter or be anything but her natural critical self with him and is irritated by Caroline's highly artificial wiles and flattery. As Jane learns to her cost, Caroline is a treacherous friend.

The Gardiners Mr Gardiner is a man of good sense and good taste. He affords a living proof to Darcy that being in trade, with an unfashionable London address, is no disqualification to being a gentleman. Indeed, Darcy comes to respect him for his integrity, as well as for his practical sense, shown in the part he plays after Lydia's elopement (where he contrasts very favourably with the ineffectual Mr Bennet).

Mrs Gardiner is practical, too, and as discreet as she is perceptive about Elizabeth's feelings. She supports Jane through a difficult period, inviting her to her home, and later copes sensibly and firmly with Lydia after the elopement. Her remarks on marriage further reflect her practical wisdom, and her intuitive assessments of Wickham and Darcy are vindicated. With her husband, she makes a very favourable impression on Darcy when they meet at Pemberley, and Elizabeth, so often shamed by other members of her family, can and does feel pride in her uncle and aunt. They contrast strongly with her real father and mother and are, in effect, her spiritual parents.

4.3 STYLE

Jane Austen's prose is, by the standards of our own day, rather formal and elaborate. By the standards of her own period, it is, if anything, rather informal and far from being elaborate. This is not to deny the debt that

everyone agrees she owes to the essayists and moralists of the eighteenth
century, and in particular to Dr Johnson; but while she favours the care-
fully balanced sentences of her models and shares their liking for abstrac-
tions and certain rhetorical features such as repetition, she writes with
painstaking clarity, rarely overloading her sentences and avoiding figurative
language from distrust.

In the letters and talk of Mr Collins Jane Austen enjoys poking fun at
the excessive gravity of style to which her predecessors sometimes tended.
This is how Collins informs Mr Bennet that he wishes to heal the difference
between the two branches of the family:

> My mind however is now made up on the subject, for having received
> ordination at Easter, I have been so fortunate as to be distinguished
> by the patronage of the Right Honourable Lady Catherine de
> Bourgh, widow of Sir Lewis de Bourgh, whose bounty and benefi-
> cence has preferred me to the valuable rectory of this parish, where
> it shall be my earnest endeavour to demean myself with grateful
> respect towards her Ladyship, and be ever ready to perform those
> rites and ceremonies which are instituted by the Church of England.
> As a clergyman, moreover, I feel it my duty to promote and estab-
> lish the blessing of peace in all families within the reach of my
> influence; and on these grounds I flatter myself that my present
> overtures of good-will are highly commendable and that the circum-
> stances of my being next in the entail of Longbourn estate, will be
> kindly overlooked on your side and not lead you to reject the offer-
> ed olive branch.

The tone aimed at is clearly one of great dignity, abetted by name-dropping
and superfluous repetition ('bounty and beneficence', 'promote and
establish'); the sentences are long and heavy with subordinate clauses, and
it is significant that Mary Bennet, who makes herself ridiculous by her
pedantry, should approve their composition. But even Mary recognises
that the 'idea of the olive branch is not wholly new'. It is, of course, a
sadly overworked metaphor, classical in origin, but as much a cliché as
Collins himself is a stereotype. The style here is, indeed, the revelation of
the man: its inflation perfectly reflects Collins's inflated self-importance.
Nor is it an accident that the only other classical metaphor in the novel is
used when Lady Catherine de Bourgh asks Elizabeth, 'Are the shades of
Pemberley to be thus polluted?' The hyperbole exactly matches its speaker;
and it is significant that such exaggeration in style is confined to characters
who are themselves so exaggerated as to be caricatures. Jane Austen

exploits such pomp and excess in style for our amusement; but in order to do so, she has to stand well clear of it herself.

Most of the novel's characters have distinctive speech styles. Almost everything Mr Bennet says is tartly epigrammatic, very much in contrast with the inane volubility of his wife. Lydia Bennet speaks and writes ungrammatically, since she is uneducated and couldn't care less. Jane Bennet's speech is simpler, more direct and far less sparkling than Elizabeth's. Bingley is typically casual, while Darcy, particularly in the first half of the novel, is stiff and formal in almost all he says, and to the end speaks with a seriousness and gravity that Elizabeth respects, but has hopes of leavening with more of her own sparkle and lightness of touch. The Gardiners, predictably, speak with clarity, good sense and discretion. Jane Austen has a remarkably fine ear for tone and dialogue, especially affected and pretentious dialogue, through which her irony constantly operates. The complex and dramatic interplay of the characters' styles, together with our being far more *comprehensively* aware of them than they are of each other, provides us with rich entertainment. It also provides us with a perspective on the novel's entire action – a perspective that is at one and the same time ironic and moral.

Jane Austen herself recognised the 'playfulness and epigrammatism of the general style' of *Pride and Prejudice*. Evidence of this is there in the opening sentence:

> It is a truth universally acknowledged, that a single man in possession of a good fortune must be in want of a wife.

This is epigrammatic and arresting. It has a dignified ring to it. But before we reach the end of Chapter 1, we are ironically aware that the Bennets are no advertisement for marriage and that Mrs Bennet's scheming reflects degradingly on the dignity of such an opening.

We have noted instances of hyperbole, but there are equally playful instances of understatement. For example, it is said of Mr Bennet:

> To his wife he was very little otherwise indebted, than as her ignorance and folly had contributed to his amusement.

This is neatly said, and we have repeatedly witnessed what it claims. But the sentence that follows is powerfully charged with an irony of understatement that we enjoy at Mr Bennet's expense:

> This is not the sort of happiness which a man would in general wish to owe to his wife. . .

Sometimes Jane Austen will satirise a character or undo an apparently innocent and neutral sentence by the irony she invests in a single word. When we are told, for example, that Bingley 'felt *authorised*' by his sisters' commendation of Jane 'to think of her as he chose' (Chapter 4), we are given early warning of his having a weak character, too easily imposed on by others. Very often, words will be sarcastically loaded to mean the *opposite* of what they seem. When Elizabeth is invited by Darcy to join him and the Bingley sisters in their walk in the avenue (Chapter 10), she protests:

> No, no; stay where you are. You are charmingly grouped. . .

The word 'charmingly' stands at the opposite extreme to what Elizabeth feels, and we know it. Similarly, we know that when Mr Bennet delightedly expects Collins to 'shine', the 'shining' will not relate to his brilliance, but his fatuity.

A more complex interplay of irony involving words used in a sense opposite to their ordinary meanings occurs in this brief exchange between Elizabeth and her father:

> . . . 'So, Lizzy', said he one day, 'your sister is crossed in love, I find. I congratulate her. Next to being married, a girl likes to be crossed in love a little now and then. It is something to think of, and gives her a sort of distinction among her companions. When is your turn to come? You will hardly bear to be long outdone by Jane. Now is your time. Here are officers enough at Meryton to disappoint all the young ladies in the country. Let Wickham be *your* man. He is a pleasant fellow, and would jilt you creditably.'
>
> 'Thank you, sir, but a less agreeable man would satisfy me. We must not all expect Jane's good fortune.' (Chapter 24)

We can immediately identify 'congratulate', 'likes', 'distinction', 'outdone', 'disappoint', 'pleasant', 'creditably' and 'good fortune' as turning upside down the words' usual meanings. It is a 'playfulness' with language that delights us, but our amused satisfaction here depends upon our feeling for the characters themselves. This is an entertaining exchange between a father and daughter who love one another and show their affection, not overtly, but in appreciating and matching one another's irony and wit. No other members of the Bennet family share this bond that exists between Elizabeth and her father.

Finally, an instance of playfulness that, at the deepest level, is highly serious. When Elizabeth reveals her true feelings for Darcy, Jane asks her how long she has loved him. Elizabeth gives bantering replies, refuses to be serious, and declares:

> . . .I believe I must date it [her love for Darcy] from my first seeing his beautiful grounds at Pemberley. (Chapter 59)

Only *after* this is it said that Elizabeth gives Jane a serious reply. Certainly, at face value, what Elizabeth says about falling in love with Darcy once she saw his splendid home is an evasive joke. But the reader recalls (as Jane cannot) how when Elizabeth did in fact first see the grounds at Pemberley, she reflected quite seriously that 'to be mistress of Pemberley might be something' (Chapter 43). Elizabeth was, in fact, warm in her admiration of Darcy's estate. But to conclude that she began to love him because of his possessions (the overt sense of her bantering reply to Jane) would be wholly wrong: we know that, unlike Charlotte Lucas, she would regard this as morally degrading. The truth, of course, is that Elizabeth, seeing the natural beauty and good taste of the landscaped estates, recognised in them a true reflection of their owner's *moral* qualities; and *this* brings her to recognise the possibility of her loving Darcy.

Our appreciation of Jane Austen's style can never be adequate until we come to realise how much complex meaning can be concentrated in what an inattentive reader may pass over as a merely flippant remark. Nothing in Jane Austen's novels is there by negligence; she revised constantly and was a highly self-conscious stylist. In *Pride and Prejudice* her ironic wit ripples through dialogue and narrative alike, but finally it is integrated into the whole structure of the novel: it is a pervasive force, helping to shape dramatic action and to provide a moral perspective on that action.

5 SPECIMEN PASSAGE AND COMMENTARY

'And this,' cried Darcy, as he walked with quick steps across the room, 'is your opinion of me! This is the estimation in which you hold me! I thank you for explaining it so fully. My faults, according to this calculation, are heavy indeed! But perhaps,' added he, stopping in his walk, and turning towards her, 'these offences might have been overlooked, had not your pride been hurt by my honest confession of the scruples that had long prevented my forming any serious design. These bitter accusations might have been suppressed, had I, with greater policy, concealed my struggles, and flattered you into the belief of my being impelled by unqualified, unalloyed inclination; by reason, by reflection, by every thing. But disguise of every sort is my abhorrence. Nor am I ashamed of the feelings I related. They were natural and just. Could you expect me to rejoice in the inferiority of your connections? To congratulate myself on the hope of relations, whose condition in life is so decidedly beneath my own?

Elizabeth felt herself growing more angry every moment; yet she tried to the utmost to speak with composure when she said,

'You are mistaken, Mr Darcy, if you suppose that the mode of your declaration affected me in any other way, than as it spared me the concern which I might have felt in refusing you, had you behaved in a more gentleman-like manner.'

She saw him start at this, but he said nothing, and she continued,

'You could not have made me the offer of your hand in any possible way that would have tempted me to accept it.'

Again his astonishment was obvious; and he looked at her with an expression of mingled incredulity and mortification. She went on:

'From the very beginning, from the first moment, I may almost say, of my acquaintance with you, your manners impressing me with the fullest belief of your arrogance, your conceit, and your selfish disdain of the feelings of others, were such as to form that ground-work of disapprobation, on which succeeding events have built so immoveable a dislike; and I had not known you a month before I felt that you were the last man in the world whom I could ever be prevailed on to marry.'

'You have said quite enough, madam. I perfectly comprehend your feelings, and have now only to be ashamed of what my own have been. Forgive me for having taken up so much of your time, and accept my best wishes for your health and happiness.'

And with these words he hastily left the room, and Elizabeth heard him the next moment open the front door and quit the house. The tumult of her mind was now painfully great. She knew not how to support herself, and from actual weakness sat down and cried for half an hour. Her astonishment, as she reflected on what had passed, was increased by every review of it. That she should receive an offer of marriage from Mr Darcy! that he should have been in love with her for so many months! so much in love as to wish to marry her in spite of all the objections which had made him prevent his friend's marrying her sister, and which must appear at least with equal force in his own case, was almost incredible! It was gratifying to have inspired unconsciously so strong an affection. But his pride, his abominable pride, his shameless avowal of what he had done with respect to Jane, his unpardonable assurance in acknowledging, though he could not justify it, and the unfeeling manner in which he had mentioned Mr Wickham, his cruelty towards whom he had not attempted to deny, soon overcame the pity which the consideration of his attachment had for a moment excited. (Chapter 34)

The passage quoted above comes from the chapter in which Elizabeth Bennet, alone in Hunsford parsonage, is surprised by a visit from Darcy, who proceeds to astonish her still more by making her a proposal of marriage. When he intrudes on her, she is reading Jane's letters, 'as if intending to exasperate herself as much as possible against Mr Darcy'.

Jane Austen is admired for her irony, and here we have a supreme instance of it. The hero, all too confident of success, comes to declare his passion for someone who is in the very act of working up resentment against him and is convinced that he both despises her and is her implacable enemy! No proposal could be more thoroughly, and more dramatically, doomed. The passage follows immediately on Elizabeth's rejection of Darcy, whose agitation is captured not only by his walking 'with quick steps across the room', but by his cries of exclamation: 'And this . . . is your opinion of me! This is the estimation in which you hold me!' Such exclamations are in their nature fragmentary, spontaneous and unordered, and for this reason they contrast all the more notably with Darcy's habitual speech, which is grave and measured. It is as if Darcy's mind cannot at first grasp Elizabeth's hostility towards him, and it is only after 'stopping in his walk' and collecting himself that he is able to resume his mastery of orderly sentence-structure. Meanwhile, he refuses to answer the accusations Elizabeth has levelled against him: that he has damaged her sister's chances of marrying Bingley, and behaved badly towards Wickham. Darcy, in fact, is too proud either to protest his innocence or to offer the least account of his actions. He is satisfied *in himself* that he has not behaved improperly, just as he knows *in himself* that he has been more than fair to Wickham, and his pride is such that when he thinks his conscience is clear, he disdains explanation, expecting other people to accept his simple denial of a thing out of respect for his honour and integrity. 'My faults, according to this calculation, are heavy indeed!' is *all* he is willing to say in answer to Elizabeth's direct challenge. Disdaining either apology or explanation, he retreats into laconic sarcasm.

It is only after 'stopping in his walk' (the author's intrusion into the highly dramatic dialogue reads like a stage direction), that Darcy can establish a reason for his humiliating rejection, and when he alleges that Elizabeth has nursed grievances against him out of her own hurt pride, irony reaches its peak. Elizabeth's 'bitter accusations' are denied validity on the grounds that they are made out of resentment at his 'honest confession of the scruples' that for so long kept him from declaring his love for someone whose relations' 'condition in life is so decidedly beneath [his] own'. If he musters sufficient delicacy here to speak of Elizabeth's relations, rather than directly of Elizabeth herself, it is as far as he is willing to go in making concessions. Very far from accepting blame, he puts blame squarely on her, and does so by accusing her of the very pride she so vigorously resents in him. In his own eyes, he has been no more than honest, and the sentences in which he protests his honesty are as short, abrupt and strong as they are dogmatic. Instead of flattering Elizabeth and disguising the social gulf between them, he declares he has done her the greater honour of frankly acknowledging the struggle he has had to bring himself to the point of proposing marriage to her. Yet in the very act of accusing her of pride, he actually flaunts his own. This is evident from his rhetorical questions, enquiring with biting sarcasm whether he is expected to 'rejoice' in Elizabeth's inferior connections and to 'congratulate' himself on the prospect of making them his own. But his pride is not merely pride in his own family and superior social standing: he believes it to be *moral*, too. He claims he abhors every kind of deceit and maintains his feelings have been 'natural and just'. So far from allowing the truth of her criticisms, he cites them as a proof of his integrity.

The explanation of how Darcy can have so thoroughly misunderstood his relations with Elizabeth as to make his condescending proposal resides to a large extent in his own character and his absorption with himself. From shortly after his first seeing her, he has been more and more attracted to Elizabeth against his better judgement. He has admitted to himself her physical attraction for him, but made no effort to understand Elizabeth herself. He has admired her 'fine eyes', but failed to reckon with her as a person. Throughout half the novel, right up to this climax, he imagines he has been moving closer to Elizabeth. His growing affection for her has been so real for him, that in his self-absorbed way he has taken it for granted that she *must* be aware of his feelings, when in fact she has moved steadily further and further away from him, in mounting antagonism. Jane Austen is a master of irony of phrasing, of local instances of irony, as here when she has Darcy of all people accuse Elizabeth of pride; but this irony of an accumulating misunderstanding between hero and heroine that reaches its dramatic climax half way through the novel is irony on the largest scale. It is irony built into the design of the whole novel, and inseparable from the plot.

This large-scale irony, brought to a head in this passage, requires fully as great a misunderstanding on Elizabeth's part as on Darcy's. She has been given many indications of his increasing regard for her. He has been unable to take his eyes off her; his attentions and compliments to her have markedly increased; he keeps meeting her when she goes on walks, and Charlotte Lucas has even declared openly that Darcy must be in love with her. Yet his proposal takes her wholly by surprise! Why this should be can be answered at different levels. Though she affected to laugh off Darcy's snub at the Meryton ball, references back to this original offence have been constantly repeated, chapter after chapter, and are central to the passage we are examining: his 'arrogance', 'conceit' and 'selfish disdain of the feelings of others' date back, she insists, to 'the first moment' of their relationship. Everything points to her having been hurt. It follows from this that she is so prejudiced against Darcy that she misinterprets all his subsequent attempts to make up to her, so that *her* absorption with her own resentful feelings blinds her to him quite as much as his self-absorption has blinded him to her. She has ignored all evidence in his favour, while crediting all evidence against him.

So far as it goes, this is all very well; but much more lies beneath it. It is possible to argue that Elizabeth's hostility towards Darcy is fuelled by her love for Jane and her generous impulses towards Wickham, both of whom she believes he has injured. We can balance Darcy's too-concentrated concern for himself with Elizabeth's self-centred belief that because her feelings of hostility are so real to herself, Darcy cannot but reciprocate them. But even this ignores her stated and *conscious* 'determination' to hate Darcy (Chapter 18). The clue to Elizabeth's relationship with Darcy lies not at all in her conscious hostility to him, but in how this conscious hostility relates to what is happening inside her at a more profound, unconscious level. The theme, running right through the story, of appearances in conflict with as underlying reality, is given its subtlest and most ironic twists in the mistaken views that both hero and heroine entertain, not simply about each other, but about themselves.

Darcy's original snub, which Elizabeth at first affected to think funny, is again raised here, but accusingly, and in deadly earnest, to explain her 'immovable' dislike. She has clearly received much more than a flesh wound; and what follows is a highly significant revelation:

> . . .I had not known you a month before I felt that you were the last man in the world whom I could ever be prevailed on to marry.

If only Darcy had been calmer, he might have replied, very cogently, that since at this early stage of their relationship neither he nor any one else had entertained the idea of 'prevailing' on her to marry him, what she says here is both gratuitous and revealing. If, moreover, he had been afforded the insights of modern psychology, he would certainly have taken heart, not simply from what she says (though it is tantamount to a betraying confession), but from the anger with which it is said, from the extravagant terms used when she denies that she could have been tempted by his offering his hand 'in any possible way', and from her assertion that he is 'the last man in the world' she could be persuaded to marry.

Today, we are much more aware than our ancestors were of the ambiguous nature of feelings, particularly of strong feelings, and even if we have never read so much as a book on psychology, we are familiar with the expression 'love-hate relationship' and what it implies. The growing anger Elizabeth feels, the flinging back in Darcy's face of the deep hurt she first received at his hands, her preoccupation with putting him down, her hitting back at him where it hurts most, accusing him of failing to behave in a 'gentleman-like manner', all point in one direction. Her 'determination' to dislike him can then be seen as an attempt to evade facing her own emotions and so to escape from a self-knowledge she finds threatening. The passage drives home our awareness that Elizabeth has been and is *emotionally* involved with Darcy in a way she never has been with either Wickham or Fitzwilliam. The psychologically significant thing is the depth and strength of her involvement, not its being negative.

Darcy, affronted by the apparent extremity of Elizabeth's dislike, regains composure by falling back on an artificial formality, and takes his leave by asking her to 'accept [his] best wishes for [her] health and happiness'. Whether this formula is as polite as it sounds is open to doubt. It could be spoken meaninglessly, or even with a touch of sarcasm; it could refer back to his excuse for coming to see her (she has a headache) or just possibly indicate, as the conclusion of the letter he sends her does, that despite her treatment of him, he still cares for her. Jane Austen's art creates a fictive reality so complex that like life itself, it is open to varying possibilities of interpretation.

Once Darcy leaves her, Elizabeth's reactions further confirm what has been said concerning her lack of self-knowledge about her profoundest feelings. The 'tumult of her mind' is 'painfully great', and though not at all the fainting type, she very nearly faints. Just as Darcy is shocked into exclamations by discovering her anger, she is now shocked into exclamations by the discovery of his love for her. Short bursts of exclamation convey, as formal sentences cannot, her emotional state. That so important a man should love her, and that he should have done so for so long, and 'in spite of all the objections which had made him prevent his friend's marrying her sister', astonishes her, of course; but it also flatters and pleases her to have 'inspired unconsciously so strong an affection'. She cries, significantly enough, 'for half an hour'. This is her first and spontaneous reaction to Darcy's proposal, once she is left alone, and only a totally imperceptive reader could now believe her violent objections to him can be taken at their face value.

Her second, more conscious and rational reaction is to fall back into condemning Darcy for 'abominable pride', blaming him for the acknowledged part he has played in separating Bingley from Jane and for his 'unpardonable assurance' in refusing to apologise for his 'cruel' treatment of Wickham. In this way, Elizabeth can persist in her determination to dislike Darcy and so stave off emotions she does not even begin properly to understand. We, as readers, are fully aware that her hurt pride, shrewdly perceived by Darcy, and her unremitting prejudice have badly misled her, and that her judgement, on which she particularly prides herself, will suffer further correction in future.

By the supreme skill of the author, we are sympathetically involved in the distorting perceptions of *both* the hero and heroine, but we are able to transcend their partial and subjective judgements in our more objective and comprehensive awareness of all that is taking place in the novel. From this climactic point on, hero and heroine, having exposed their total misunderstanding of one another and of themselves, will set in reverse the whole movement of the plot. Very gradually, they will begin to draw closer to each other, substituting understanding for misunderstanding, self-knowledge for pride, and sympathy for prejudice. The passage examined is the fulcrum point of the novel's entire action.

6 CRITICAL RECEPTION

The critical attention given to *Pride and Prejudice* on its publication was in general favourable and encouraging. In the *British Critic*, February 1813, the anonymous reviewer has confidence enough to declare:

> It [*Pride and Prejudice*] is very far superior to almost all the publications of the kind which have lately come before us. It has a very unexceptionable tendency, the story is well told, the characters remarkably well drawn and supported, and written with great spirit as well as vigour.

But there is little analysis to back up this judgement, and the 'very unexceptionable tendency' of the story (its rectitude in tone and content) is what primarily commends it to the reviewer. Literary judgements at this period were generally subordinated to *moral* considerations, as a second anonymous reviewer, writing in the March 1813 issue of the *Critical Review*, clearly testifies:

> An excellent lesson may be learned from the elopement of Lydia:— the work also shows the folly of letting young girls have their own way, and the danger which they incur in associating with the officers, who may be quartered in or near their residence.

The expectation was that a novel should be didactic, and the review is typically preoccupied with the positive practical benefits afforded by the novel:

> The line she [Jane Austen] draws between the prudent and the mercenary in matrimonial concerns, may be useful to our fair readers. . .

In a private letter, Annabella Milbanke, who was later to marry Lord Byron, places *Pride and Prejudice* neatly within its literary background, and is among the first to recognise its domestic realism as an outstanding virtue:

> I have finished the novel. . .which I think a very superior work. It depends not on any of the common resources of novel writers, no drownings, no conflagrations, nor runaway horses, nor lap-dogs and parrots, no chambermaids and milliners, nor rencontres and disguises. I really think it is the *most probable* I have ever read. (1813)

In 1826, Sir Walter Scott, himself a hugely celebrated and popular novelist, acknowledged that his 'Big Bow-wow strain' of writing (writing that tends to heroic or melodramatic exaggeration) was legitimately challenged by 'the exquisite touch' of *Pride and Prejudice*, 'which renders ordinary commonplace things and characters interesting from the truth of the description. . .'. His tribute to the book is all the more generous because its excellence is of a completely different kind from that of his own fiction:

> Also read again and for the third time at least Miss Austen's very finely written novel of *Pride and Prejudice*. That young lady had a talent for describing the involvement and feelings and characters of ordinary life which is to me the most wonderful I ever met with.

But the same domestic realism praised by Scott and others was held in disdain, if not contempt, by another celebrated and popular novelist, Charlotte Brontë. Writing in 1848 to George Henry Lewes, the philosopher and critic who had praised *Pride and Prejudice* for its fine construction, the 'ease and naturalness' of its story, and the way in which 'characters, scenes and dialogue' are so economically and perfectly integrated, she takes him severely to task for preferring Jane Austen's limitations to Scott's romantic extravagance. Provoked by Lewes's praise into reading *Pride and Prejudice* for the first time, she writes:

> . . .I got the book. And what did I find? An accurate daguerrotyped portrait of a commonplace face; a carefully fenced, highly cultivated garden, with neat borders and delicate flowers; but no glance of a bright, vivid physiognomy, no open country, no fresh air, no blue hill, no bonny beck. I should hardly like to live with her ladies and gentlemen, in their elegant but confined houses.

Clearly, Charlotte Brontë, unlike Scott, found it hard to admire a genius so very different from her own, which was often exaggeratedly romantic and melodramatic. If we accept her metaphor of *Pride and Prejudice* as a fenced and artificial garden, her own novels, by implication, are to be regarded, like the Yorkshire moors in which she grew up, as wild expanses of elevating and untamed nature.

Though there will always be some readers who agree with Charlotte Brontë, finding the deliberately imposed limitations of *Pride and Prejudice* constraining, or even stifling and claustrophobic, twentieth-century criticism has tended to uphold Lewes's high evaluation of the work, often on the grounds of artistic accomplishment he drew particular attention to. This is well exemplified by Mary Lascelles's study, significantly called *Jane Austen and Her Art*. What fascinated Lascelles is precisely Jane Austen's contrived craftsmanship. *Pride and Prejudice* she claims is:

> . . .deliberately shaped; its pattern shows a. . .delight in the sym-metry of correspondence and antithesis; but there is a notable difference in the contrivance. This pattern is formed by diverging and converging lines, by the movement of two people who are impel-led apart until they reach a climax of mutual hostility, and thereafter bend their courses towards mutual understanding and sympathy.
>
> (1939)

Another critic, Reuben A. Brower, considers the prose, and especially the dialogue, of *Pride and Prejudice* to be as concentrated and rewarding as great satirical poetry:

> As in our reading of Pope, we may. . .appreciate the extraordinary richness of ironic texture and the imaginative continuity running through the play of wit. In analysing the ironies and the assumptions, we shall see how intensely dramatic the dialogue is, dramatic in the sense of defining characters through the way they speak and are spoken about. (*The Fields of Light*, 1951)

While it is true to say that her artistic skills have led to the steadily increas-ing reputation of Jane Austen throughout the twentieth century, in America quite as much as in Britain, we should by no means neglect the hold *Pride and Prejudice* continues to have for readers interested in the delights and dangers of courtship and marriage in Regency society. The *themes* of *Pride and Prejudice* continue to fascinate us, just as they did her earliest readers, and in her recent book, *Jane Austen's Novels – Social Change and Literary Form*, Julia Prewitt Brown, an American scholar, shares with the earliest anonymous critics a concern for the book's moral and didactic dimensions:

Pride and Prejudice is far more preoccupied than Austen's other novels with the rituals and taboos concerning mating. In the course of the novel four marriages are decided: those of Charlotte Lucas, Lydia, Jane and Elizabeth; five, if we include Colonel and Mrs Foster. Every social event is important in affecting the attachments that will result and in forwarding the heroine's education in proper selection. There is neither cynicism nor triviality in thinking these events important; selecting a mate was the arena in which women's whole future was decided. The heroine is the last to be engaged, for part of her knowledge in selection comes through observing her friend and her sisters choose. (1979)

Finally, it should be said that while there can be wrong or perverse readings of *Pride and Prejudice* (Charlotte Brontë is perverse in making pre-conditional demands on the novel instead of submitting herself to what it has to offer), there can be no single 'correct' reading of it. A great work of literature is sufficiently complex to admit a variety of approaches and readings, and the preoccupations of different critics will lead to quite legitimate differences of interpretation and evaluation. It follows that *Pride and Prejudice* can be legitimately admired for various reasons – for its characterisation and psychological truth, for its social insights, for its satire and wit, or for its artistic achievements; or indeed, for any of the many possible combinations of these elements!

REVISION QUESTIONS

1. Discuss the theme of marriage in *Pride and Prejudice*.

2. 'One has got all the goodness, and the other all the appearance of it.' Discuss Elizabeth's comment on Darcy and Wickham.

'. . .intricate characters are the *most* interesting.' Do you agree?

What has *Pride and Prejudice* to say about parents and their responsibilities?

Right up to Darcy's proposal, the hero and heroine are moving further away from one another; after it, the reverse is true. Discuss.

Most of our amusement in reading *Pride and Prejudice* comes from our being aware of differences between appearance and reality that go unperceived by the characters themselves. Discuss and illustrate this.

The irony and satire of *Pride and Prejudice* are a testimony to the moral sanity of its author. Do you agree?

Discuss the effectiveness and range of the dialogue in *Pride and Prejudice*.

FURTHER READING

A Recommended Text is published by Macmillan (1982), edited by Raymond Wilson, for The Macmillan Students' Novels series. It contains a short critical Introduction and Notes.

Bush, Douglas, *Jane Austen* (Macmillan, 1975).

Gillie, Christopher, *A Preface to Jane Austen* (Longman, 1974).

Lascelles, Mary, *Jane Austen and her Art* (Clarendon Press, 1939).

Southam, B. C., *Sense and Sensibility, Pride and Prejudice and Mansfield Park* (Casebook Series: Macmillan, 1976).

Wright, Andrew H., *Jane Austen's Novels* (Chatto and Windus, 1953).